A Journey of Faith in the Messiness of Life

SKIPPING STONES

D. Paul Barnes

CHICAGO SPECTRUM PRESS
LOUISVILLE, KENTUCKY 40207

CHICAGO SPECTRUM PRESS
4824 BROWNSBORO CENTER
LOUISVILLE, KENTUCKY 40207
800-594-5190

Printed in the U.S.A.

10 9 8 7 6 5 4 3 2 1

ISBN: 978-1-58374-195-5

Library of Congress Cataloging-in-Publication Data:

2008939977

DEDICATION

To the One who is able to clean up the messiness of my life
and

To Char, who has lived with the mess and loved me anyway

CONTENTS

WELCOME TO SKIPPING STONES 7

PROLOGUE: DEATH BEFORE LIFE 17

STORM CLOUDS 21

I WAS A CUTE LITTLE KID 25

MAKE LOVE NOT WAR 31

    Reflection #1: Evangelicals 37

    Reflection #2: Born Again 43

A DOUBLE-EDGED SWORD 49

HAPPINESS 61

EMBRACING YOUR LIMP 69

THE DREAM KILLER 81

THE CALL 91

INTEGRITY, SIN AND GRACE 103

    Introduction 106

    Integrity 107

    Sin 110

    Grace 112

    Conclusion 114

RESIGNATION 117

FIFTEEN MINUTES OF FAME 127

    Reflection #3: The Great Divide 139

    Reflection #4: To All My Fellow Strugglers 146

Reflection #5: The Labradoodle 153

THE OFFICE 159

THE FOG 165

Reflection #6: Skipping Stones 171

Reflection #7: The Shelter 182

Reflection #8: One-Way To Heaven,

Half-A-Million Ways To Hell 189

ENGEDI 203

THE HARBOR 213

Final Thoughts: A Drop of Ink 223

Welcome to Skipping Stones

I NEVER THOUGHT I'D WRITE a book. Over the years people have asked if I'd ever considered writing and I'd always answer, "No." I'm a speaker, not a writer. One of the ways that pastors can move into writing is to have a ghost writer spruce up their sermons and get them published. But that just wasn't my style. So writing a book was not something I'd ever given much consideration.

Until now. Even now one of the things I wonder is, "Do I have within me, what it takes to write even *one* decent book?" I liken it to musicians. Some bands and singers have a string of hit songs that people enjoy while others become known as "one-hit wonders." I think authors often fall into those same two categories. I'm amazed how prolific some can be—they never seem to have a shortage of subjects to write about. Others are destined to be nothing more than one-book authors. It remains to be seen if I can earn that title or if this endeavor is nothing more than a waste of a beautiful tree.

Life is messy. At least that's been my experience. Very few people seem to make it through unscathed. We face many challenges as we journey through this world. But I *am* a person of faith, so even in the midst of the chaos and confusion, I choose to believe some things about God, others, myself, and my circumstances, that foster hope and perhaps bring some sense of purpose to all this untidiness.

Skipping Stones chronicles the messiness of my journey and my ultimate disgraceful downfall. A brief synopsis of my life would be as follows: I have been married for 31 years to a wonderful woman named Char; we have two married daughters who bring tremendous joy to our lives (as do their husbands); I am an evangelical Christian; I was a successful pastor for almost thirty years, and up until recently I lived with a closely guarded secret that ultimately became my undoing: I struggle with homosexuality.

The wording of that last phrase is important: I struggle with homosexuality. As an evangelical Christian I have trouble simply writing off homosexuality as being "born that way." Granted, many do take that approach and in a multitude of ways it can make life a whole lot less messy. However, my faith keeps me from adopting that attitude. Believe me—there have been many times when I wish I could. However, as one who has spent a lifetime trying to understand the dynamics of human sexuality, I view the position that a person is born gay as somewhat of a simplistic cop out. Not that it doesn't have some merit, but putting that slant on this issue shuts down any honest and deep introspection which would attempt to understand the many multifaceted issues behind the sexual preference. Do I believe there is a biological component to homosexuality? Yes. But there is more to it than that. There are also sociological and psychological pieces to this puzzle; thus it becomes an extremely complex issue.

For those who struggle with homosexuality and agree with what I've just written, you'll understand the depth of my torment as I've tried to deal with my sexuality. My situation (like many others I've discovered) is made even more complicated because of my faith, my marriage, and my profession. For those who have already had their anger aroused because you *don't* agree with me—that's O.K.

My purpose isn't to start a debate or try to win one. I would simply ask that you hear me out. This book is not an attempt to prove any particular viewpoint regarding a person's sexual orientation. Rather, it is the story of my personal struggle. My struggle with my sexuality and my faith, the tremendous tension those two things have created, and the ramifications I've had to live with in trying to reconcile them. *Regardless* of how you view homosexuality, the reality for most men and women who deal with it in their lives is that it is not without conflict and heartache. On that point, perhaps we can agree.

Over the years I've engaged in homosexual behavior. In doing so I broke my marriage vows, and been dishonest with my wife, children, and the church I served. As if that isn't severe enough, because of my belief system, I've also dishonored God. Consequently, I've lived my life under the shadowy umbrella of numerous dark emotions: guilt, remorse, fear, apprehension, shame, embarrassment, confusion, uncertainty, and doubt. I've felt like Joe Bfstplk. Joe, with his vowel-challenged unpronounceable name, was a character in Al Capp's comic strip, *Li'l Abner*. He was a tiny little man who wore a ragged wide brim hat. His trademark however, was a black cloud that hovered over his head and followed him wherever he went. My black cloud has produced a continual downpour of emotions that have caused me to travel through life over some very slippery ground.

Another consequence of hiding my secret has been loneliness. I've lived a very lonely life, but not in the way one might think. In many ways, life has been very full. Fortunately, I have my best friend in the world living under the same roof with me—my wife. In that regard, I am very fortunate. Our daughters and their husbands are terrific and we have wonderful times with them. We've taken many memorable vacations and connected with a handful of people along the road of life who have become true friends. Over the years we've also had a few family pets that have brought a lot of life into our home. Currently we have a Maltese puppy named Phoenix (he looks like a six pound polar bear) who loves to sit in my lap and chew on my fingers. He's good for a few laughs every day.

The loneliness I'm referring to is something more personal, something that is deep within. It's a loneliness that comes from the core *being* of an individual. Mark Twain said, "The worst loneliness is not to be comfortable with yourself." I don't know if Mr. Twain personally experienced this or if it was just another stroke of his genius, but he hit the nail on the head with that comment. I understand it—perfectly. It's been a challenge for me to like me *for* me. Being comfortable in my own skin has not been something I've experienced very often in my life, and that truly is loneliness.

Secrets also make relationships difficult. When there is an issue in your life of which you are ashamed and afraid to share, you develop a number of defense mechanisms aimed at keeping people from discovering that secret. A person is never really sure how another will respond if the secret is discovered. The most ideal response of course, is acceptance and love, but it could be rejection, judgment, disgust, contempt, or condemnation. Naturally that leads to lot of "arms-length" associations. Recently, I ran into a couple I knew while I was out shopping. The husband was cordial, but his wife wouldn't even acknowledge my greeting or look me in the eyes. In order to avoid those kinds of reactions, you learn to keep your secret a secret.

Being a follower of Jesus Christ has also made life incredibly challenging. I'll address this issue later on, but the Christian community has an interesting approach to behaviors they determine to be sinful. Jesus traced all sinful behavior to the heart of a man or woman. He said, "For out of the heart come evil thoughts, murder, adultery, sexual immorality, theft, false testimony, slander."[1] It's because of what's going on inside us that ultimately causes us to behave in ways that can be harmful to ourselves or others.

For example, Jesus said, "I tell you that anyone who looks at a woman lustfully has already committed adultery with her in his heart."[2] When thought about logically, that would mean that every single one of us has pondered things in our hearts that would be wrong. But as long as simply *thinking* about evil things is all we do, the Christian community takes a hands-off approach. Once we *act* on those thoughts however, a line is crossed and some kind of appropriate action needs to be taken against the individual. Having spent my adult life in the church, I have lived with a very sobering awareness of just what happens when bad behavior is discovered.

My internal struggle with homosexuality and then acting on those desires, rather than being something that could be dealt with behind the private, closed doors of the family home, became national news—my fifteen minutes of fame, I guess you could say. Fortunately, people's memories are pretty short and all the hoopla passed very quickly, but the ramifications my family and I have had to live with are long-lasting.

However, since it did become so public, I feel it is now time to share some thoughts on my life, the Christian faith which I embrace, the church which gives me both joy and heartache, and the countless numbers of men and women who have to deal with their own struggle as they try to integrate their sexuality and their spirituality. My heart hurts so much for them.

This is a book about *process*, not about *conclusion*. Conclusions always speak of finality to me. Of, "This is the end of the story." Usually the story has a happy ending. All of us love our fairy tales that end with the line, "And they all lived happily ever after." But since my life is in process, this is a process book. It's about my story, my journey through light and darkness, through fear and hope, through rejection and acceptance. And I'll tell you right now so you don't have to go to the last page to find out, the conclusion is—I'm still on the journey. As yet, the ending has not been written.

In many ways, that seems very natural to me. Every one of us is on a journey through life. Our voyage doesn't really end until we die. So, when we're telling our personal story, any conclusions before that seem premature. The fact is none of us knows what the next chapter of our life will be. We don't know what good things or bad things will happen to us as we transition from one season of life into a new one, or what lies waiting for us around the next corner. Life is all about embracing the unknown of a thousand tomorrows, and doing it with the confident assurance that Someone is traveling with us through those uncharted waters.

Who is this book for? I met with an agent early on in this process to see what was involved in getting a book to market. He said I needed to identify my audience. To whom did I want to speak? As I thought about a few of the books I've read lately that impacted me the most, I realized it was hard to narrow down their target group. In some ways, that's how I feel about this book. My story ties everything together but as my story unfolds, my thoughts cover a lot of territory.

Within these pages you'll find chapters about me, my insecurities and dreams, faith, times of darkness and despair, glimmers of hope and encouragement, observations of people, and what I think is really important in today's world. You'll find thoughts about the church, and how discouraged I am that so many Christians don't seem to be getting the basic message of Christianity. For lack of a better term, I simply call these chapters a REFLECTION— my observations on issues of spirituality as I see them today.

Initially this project was to benefit no one but myself. I was writing for *me*. I was in turmoil and needed to get the jumbled thoughts out of my brain and some of the roller-coaster emotions out of my heart. Over the months as I continued to write, I began to realize it had the potential to be something more. I became aware of three different audiences with whom I would like to try and connect.

I wish Christian leaders would read this book. I hope that something I write will prompt the leaders of the Christian movement to think a little differently about church and how we do church and what is involved in helping Christ-followers develop genuine spirituality. There is a huge difference between Christianity and spirituality. The fact of the matter is what we're doing right now to try to help Christians develop their spirituality isn't working. It hasn't worked for a number of decades. We need some dialogue on what needs to change in order to see genuine, spiritual vitality blossom in people's lives.

I hope the average Christian sitting in the pews of churches will read this book. What I've discovered through my journey is that the vast majority of Christians have a family member or friend who identifies himself or herself as being "gay." Yet most don't really seem to understand the dynamics of human sexuality. Many simply write it off as, "Well, they're sinning. They need to repent of their sin and let God heal them." In my view, that's simplistic and trite, very judgmental, and not at all loving. I hope something I write will be a bridge of understanding and compassion from the Christian community to those who feel alienated from Christ because of the way the Christian community has responded to this issue in the last few decades.

Finally, I wish that some secular, skeptical, yet searching men and women will read this book. The pull of spirituality tugs at the heartstrings of all people—those who have already embraced some kind of faith and those who are still on their own journey of spiritual discovery. I call people who have not yet embraced a faith in Jesus Christ but who are searching for answers, sojourners. A sojourner is a person who comes to a place, stays for a brief visit, and then continues on his or her journey.

If you have picked up this book and are one of those individuals who is seeking—welcome. I'm glad you've decided to spend a little of your time with me. Perhaps something I write will help you in your journey towards God. I hope you might get a glimpse of how much love God has for you, how He longs to be in a relationship with you, and how, regardless of what you have done or how down on yourself you might be, *you* bring a great deal of joy to His heart, whether you realize it or not.

Over the years as a pastor of a church, I accumulated an extensive library. I had thousands of volumes. I've always had the thought that if I could glean just one or two good ideas from a book, then it was worth the purchase price.

If something in a book...

    caused me to think about a topic more deeply,

      challenge a conviction that I held,

        forced me to pause and spend some time in contemplation,

          or adoration,

            made me smile,

              or gave me hope,

                made me more loving, more understanding, or more kind,

  ...then it was a good read.

As you read, perhaps this will be true for you.

I received a fortune cookie once that I've kept in my billfold for years—I guess I was keeping it for this occasion. It said, "Four basic premises of writing: clarity, brevity, simplicity, and humanity." My aim has been to accomplish those four goals. I've tried to write as I think—simply. I trust I have made my thoughts clear. Most chapters in this book are relatively short. They are like reading a few pages from my personal journal. I hope that in the process of reading you will get to know me. What I would like you to know about me is that I am a human being, deeply loved by God, yet painfully aware that I have feet of clay. In the New Testament Book of James it says, "We all stumble in many ways…"[3] This book is about my stumbling. Yet I've always believed that the real measure of a man or woman isn't how many times they fall down, but how many times they pick themselves up and continue pressing on.

That's why the following quote inspires me: "It is not the critic who counts; not the man who points out how the strong man stumbles, or where the doer of deeds could have done them better. The credit belongs to the man who is actually in the arena, whose face is marred by dust and sweat and blood; who strives valiantly; who errs, who comes short again and again, because there is no effort without error and shortcoming; but who does actually strive to do the deeds; who knows great enthusiasms, the great devotions; who spends himself in a worthy cause; who at the best knows in the end the triumph of high achievement, and who at the worst, if he fails, at least fails while daring greatly, so that his place shall never be with those cold and timid souls who neither know victory nor defeat."[4]

If you are a person who likes your books to end all nicely wrapped up in a pretty little bow, be forewarned that this book is different. Because you see, I'm a sojourner, too. Even as a Christian, I'm on a continuing journey of discovery as I explore the vastness of an infinite God. You are catching me at a pit-stop. I haven't reached my final destination yet, so conclusions are few and far between.

But for those of you who are on your own journey and realize that your story isn't finished yet either—well, you and I understand each other. Maybe we will become friends through this process. Perhaps parts of my story will resonate with yours, some of my thoughts will echo ones you've been having, and my questions and deepest longings will reflect some of the issues that you've been wrestling with in your heart.

My prayer is that you will be a little stronger and a bit wiser for having spent some time journeying with me. At least I hope so.

I don't like the thought of wasting a tree.

---

[1] Matthew 15:19
[2] Matthew 5:28
[3] James 3:2
[4] "The Man in the Arena" is the title of a speech given by Teddy Roosevelt at the Sorbonne in Paris, France on April 23, 1910. It was subsequently re-printed in his book, *Citizenship in a Republic*.

Prologue

DEATH BEFORE LIFE

I DIED BEFORE I EVER HAD the chance to live. First lines of books are intriguing to me. Have you noticed how some of them work their way into the mainstream of literary history and are able to stand alone, apart from the rest of the book? "It was the best of times, it was the worst of times" from Charles Dickens's *Tale of Two Cities*. Or how about, "Call me Ishmael" from *Moby Dick* by Herman Melville. As I thought about writing a book, I realized I wanted my first line to be a memorable one. I don't know how unforgettable this first line will be for you, but it holds a great deal of significance to me.

In 1962 Pete Seeger released the song, "Turn, Turn, Turn." The first few lines of that song say,

> "To Everything (Turn, Turn, Turn)
> There is a season (Turn, Turn, Turn)
> And a time for every purpose, under Heaven
>
> A time to be born, a time to die…"

Those words have a very ancient source attached to them. King Solomon, one of the wisest men who ever lived, first penned them in the book of Ecclesiastes. Ecclesiastes 3:1-8 reads:

> "There is a time for everything,
> and a season for every activity under heaven:
>
> a time to be born and a time to die,
> a time to plant and a time to uproot,

a time to kill and a time to heal,
a time to tear down and a time to build,

a time to weep and a time to laugh,
a time to mourn and a time to dance,

a time to scatter stones and a time to gather them,
a time to embrace and a time to refrain,

a time to search and a time to give up,
a time to keep and a time to throw away,

a time to tear and a time to mend,
a time to be silent and a time to speak,

a time to love and a time to hate,
a time for war and a time for peace."

A time to be born and a time to die. In the natural order of things, birth comes before death. However, life has a way of never traveling in a straight line and for some, death actually comes before birth. That's how I've felt about my life.

Like a trickle of water that starts high in the mountains as the snow begins to melt in the spring, and then becomes a brook which turns into a stream, and finally a river which can become a torrent of raging whitewater, my life has followed a similar course. Through a combination of circumstances and events, I've traveled in a direction that has caused a lifetime of heartache and sadness.

As a child it was difficult to process the feelings I was having. As an adolescent, once puberty kicked in and the hormones started raging, life became a confusing jumble of emotions. As an adult, especially as a Christian, I've lived with continual tension. Trying to reconcile my faith with my sexuality has been incredibly frustrating. Yet I won't abandon my faith nor can I ignore my sexuality. Being married to a woman whom I love dearly, yet struggling with my sexual orientation has made life even more heartbreaking. Being a pastor and knowing that my profession and my sexual struggle were at great odds with each other threw me into the violent whitewater of conflict almost every day of my adult life.

It's hard to live effectively much less enjoy life when there is so much turmoil raging inside. I have often felt like a dead man walking. Thus I say I died before I ever had the chance to live.

Yet in the midst of all the chaos and confusion there is a thought that begs to be heard. It keeps pushing its way to the forefront of my mind and I can't escape its reality: sometimes it's necessary to die before a rebirth can take place. That's why I'm intrigued by the image of the phoenix, the bird which rose out of the ashes, reborn from flames. Coming from Egyptian mythology, the phoenix was said to live for 500 years. At the end of its life-cycle the phoenix would build itself a nest, set the nest and itself on fire, and both would be reduced to ashes. From those ashes a new, young phoenix would emerge. The bird was also said to be able to regenerate when hurt or wounded, and tears from a phoenix could heal people's wounds. It's beautiful imagery.

People's lives are a lot like that of a phoenix.

- Sometimes we have to go down in flames before we can be reborn in strength.

- Often the wounds of life hurt deeply but they are not fatal.

- And every now and then our tears become the stream from which others can drink and find healing, hope and strength for themselves as they navigate the rapids of their own life.

No two of us take identical paths. We are all as unique and different as the billions of snowflakes that fall every winter. Yet it is through our individual stories, that we and others can see how God interacts with us—how He comes into our lives and walks with us through this expedition called life. This is my story. I've crashed and burned, but I want to believe that I am like a phoenix rising. This is *my* journey.

ONE

STORM CLOUDS

IT WAS A TYPICAL Tuesday evening in December. The year was quickly drawing to a close and I was sitting in the conference room, ready for another board meeting to begin. I'll have to confess that after attending church board meetings for almost 30 years, I was getting a little tired of them. Let's see, at least twice a month and sometimes every week, each one lasting at least 2 1/2 to 3 hours, times 28 years—that adds up to over 2,000 hours, or twelve weeks, or three months of my life spent in those meetings.

Generally they were pretty typical gatherings, dealing with church finances, staffing situations, expansion plans, church member concerns, and people's needs, but this particular meeting caused my heart to race a whole lot faster than normal. During the meeting one of our elders brought an issue to the board's attention that the church receptionist had called him about. She'd received a couple of phone calls, he said. The first one was short and very direct: "I'd like to speak to your gay pastor." She said we didn't have a gay pastor and the individual hung up. A week later this same individual called again. "I'd like to speak to your gay pastor." Again she informed him that we didn't have any gay pastors. He said something I'd rather not repeat and hung up again. It rattled her. She called one of our church leaders and he brought it to the attention of our board that Tuesday evening in December. But as quickly as the issue was brought up, it was dismissed by the board as being a crank caller and we moved on to other business.

For me, however, it marked the beginning of a very sleepless night. I kept hoping that during the meeting my flushed face wouldn't give away my racing heart. But that was the night I realized something: someone was out there, some anonymous, no name person, who knew my secret and for whatever reason wanted to do me some serious harm. Ruin my life would be another way of putting it—destroying everything I'd spent my entire adult life working for.

This came on the heels of two other interesting events. Just a month or two before I'd had two intriguing conversations. I was at the gym one day and a man that I casually knew came up to me and said, "I heard you resigned your position at the church. What are you doing now?" I said, "No. I'm still there. Where did you hear that?" He thought for a moment and said, "I don't remember but all I know is someone passed that on to me." Then a few weeks later, also at the gym, another individual who was a casual acquaintance came up to me and said with a tone of true concern in his voice, "I heard you got a divorce. How are you doing?" I said "No. My wife and I are still together—almost thirty years. Where did you hear that?" Again he couldn't remember the source. But, two very disturbing comments coming within a few weeks of each other. Now the phone calls. Were they related? Who knows? But something was up. It was obvious someone was out there, who wanted to do me some serious harm. The disconcerting thing was that I couldn't do a thing about it. All of a sudden I felt very vulnerable.

I don't remember much about the rest of that meeting. All I knew was I wanted it to be over so I could get out of there. I went home and literally did not sleep at all that night. I lay in bed thinking, "This is it. The day I'd feared for years has finally come to pass." I started thinking about the fact that this would probably be my last Christmas as Pastor of Grace Chapel. I began to wonder how I would break the news to my wife Char, my kids, what I would do to keep a roof over our heads and food on the table. A million different thoughts raced through my head all night long. By the next morning, I was exhausted. I dragged myself into the office and throughout most of the day my thoughts kept coming back to the conversation from the night before. When would the other shoe drop, I kept wondering? When would this mysterious caller call again and what would he say this time?

But then, nothing happened. At least not immediately. December came and went. The new year was ushered in and while it was never far from the front of my mind, the excitement and challenges that we were facing as a church began to push that ugly fear into the background, and I found myself immersed in the day to day happenings that go along with pastoring a mega-church—well, an almost mega church.

TWO

I WAS A CUTE LITTLE KID

PICTURE THIS: A WARM summer day, a small town's community swimming pool, and a cute little five-year-old boy ready to have some fun splashing in the water. I say cute because that's what my parents always said about me. I was a cute little baby (I've got great baby pictures to prove it) and apparently I was always smiling and generally good natured. I have to take my parent's word for this since honestly I don't remember too much about those early years.

But one memory that stands out vividly was that day at the swimming pool. We were visiting my grandparents for the week. They lived in a small town in the Ozark country of Missouri—lots of lakes and trees and humidity and bugs. Snakes too. My great-grandmother lived all by herself in a little house in the middle of the woods. One summer I remember going out to visit her. After driving through the forest for what seemed like an eternity, we came to a clearing where her house was located. When we stepped out of the car, I remember hearing the rustling of snakes (*plural—snakes—lots of them*) as they slithered away in the underbrush around the house. It gave me the creeps, and fortunately we never went back there again.

But I digress. Back to the swimming pool. My dad came from a large family. He had three brothers (a fourth one had died at the age of twelve) and two sisters. Whenever we'd come to visit, all the brothers and sisters and their spouses and all their kids (my cousins—lots of them) would come together. It was reunion time, and everyone seemed to enjoy it. That particular visit my dad, his brothers, a group of my cousins, and I had all gone swimming on that hot, muggy Missouri afternoon. It was in the locker room, after we were finished, that I noticed something about myself. I was having some funny feelings as I saw these naked men getting showered and dressed. I'm sorry to be so blunt, but I don't quite know how else to put it. Something inside my stomach was fluttering and of course, as a little five year old guy, I had no idea what it was.

Years later, I would come to realize that it was on that day, that typical, just like any other summer day in Missouri, it was on that day that I died. As an innocent, cute, good natured, happy-go-lucky little five-year old, I died. You don't get a lot of living in before you're five years old. A few Christmases, riding around on your tricycle, some birthday cakes and ice cream, and that's about it. It's always made me very sad that sometimes people die before they ever have a chance to live. It seems so terribly unfair.

I'm not going to spend a lot of time telling you about my growing up. But there are three things that I think you should know that shaped or helped define me in my early years.

First of all, by nature I'm an introvert. As a boy I was very shy and always would feel inferior and out of place when I'd get around my cousins or other kids who were boisterous, loud, and outgoing. They seemed to breeze through life so much easier than I did. They could make friends easily. They could tell a good joke. They had other kids hanging around them wanting to be their friends. As an adult, because of the nature of the work I've been in, I learned a lot of skills in drawing people out, being the question-asker, making people feel comfortable while I was speaking to them, that sort of thing. So, people have been continually surprised when I tell them I'm introverted. They have a hard time believing it. But it's true. It's because of that fact, that pouring my life out onto these pages is not the easiest thing in the world to do—especially because of the very personal, intimate nature of my story.

The second thing I think you should know about my childhood is that we moved around a lot. I went to nine different schools in twelve years. My father worked in retail and every time his company would give him a promotion, they would move him. So, we never stayed in any one place very long. That was a real compliment to my dad, by the way. He was very good at what he did. But generally we'd be some place anywhere from eighteen to thirty-six months and we'd move on. That's hard on a kid who has trouble making friends in the first place because of his introverted personality. Somewhere along the line I began to realize that because we weren't going to stay around in any one place very long, it really wasn't worth trying to develop new friends—I'd just have to leave them pretty soon anyway. Consequently, I became a loner.

The third thing I'd like you to know is this: I broke my right arm three times as a kid. The first time was when I fell twelve feet out of a tree, the second time I fell off a skateboard, and the third time was when I got caught up in some kid's roller skates at a skating rink. This may seem like a funny thing to mention, but it definitely affected my growing up years. The doctor told my parents that because I'd had three compound fractures on the same arm within a very short period of time (the third time I broke it I'd only been out of the cast a week from my second break!) the nerves had been so badly damaged that if it was ever broken again, there would be a strong possibility that the arm would stop growing. Well, that's all it took for my parents to forbid me from playing sports.

So, I spent most of my entire time in junior high with casts on my arm. I'd come home from school and since I was too young to drink hard liquor, I'd drown my sorrows by pouring a big glass of Wink (a lemon-lime soda drink of a bygone era) and cook up a huge bowl of macaroni swimming in butter. I got a little plump.

In fact I'll never forget the time I was in the locker room after gym class. I had taken my shower and was sitting on the bench getting dressed when the gym teacher (who was also the school coach) came by. He leaned up against the wall across from me, looked at me and said, "You ever plan to play any sports?"

"Well, I was thinking about going out for basketball," I said.

Then with a tone of disgust in his voice he looked down at my stomach and said, "Well, you're going to have to lose a lot of that fat first."

With that he walked away. I've often wondered how it is that some people get put into the positions they do. How that man became a coach is a mystery to me. Maybe that was his way of trying to motivate me. It obviously didn't work too well, because I never tried out for the basketball team. Instead, I went home and had some more macaroni.

Once I finally got out of my cast after the third broken arm, I participated in no sports in high school. Not that I was really all that interested in too many of them, but at the same time, it's obvious who the cool kids are in high school—the jocks and the cheerleaders. Since I wasn't in either of those groups, it made for just another reason why I spent so much of my time alone.

When you're a teenager especially, one of the things that being alone does is make you feel very inferior. As a kid you're not really able to identify it as such, but somewhere in the recesses of your mind you start thinking you're the kind of person nobody likes—that you're not likeable. There must be something fundamentally wrong with you that keeps people from wanting to be your friend. So in addition to fighting with the constant zits that would dot my face, I was forever fighting with the fact that on the *inside* I felt like a zit as well.

I will never forget the first time I ever ate alone in a fast food restaurant. Up until then I would always go through the drive through and sit in the parking lot to eat my hamburger and fries. But finally I decided that I needed to go sit inside where it was cool. I thought to myself, "This is stupid, sitting outside in a hot car in the middle of the summer when there is air conditioning only a few steps away." So I went to McDonalds one day, parked the car, walked in and ordered. After I got my order I found a spot to sit down feeling incredibly self-conscious. The whole time I was sure everyone in the place was looking at me thinking, "What a loser he is. Doesn't he have any friends? Why is he here by himself? Poor guy." They were right on one account: I didn't have too many friends, but the fact of the matter was I wasn't a loser. I didn't come to realize that truth until later in life, however. That was the first of what would become count-less times that I would eat by myself. It took years before I ever felt comfortable eating alone, but after enough time passes, you do get used to it.

 THREE

MAKE LOVE NOT WAR

I ENVY PEOPLE WHO WERE born in the 1970s, 1980s and 1990s.

I call all these people "emergents." There have been a lot of terms slapped on to the generations that have come up since the Baby Boomers: the Baby Busters, Generation-X, Generation-Y, the Millennials, etc. I'll leave the discussion of the differences between these age groups to the sociologists. For my purpose here, I prefer to lump all the people who've been born since the mid-1970s into one category—the emergents. The emerging generations. Coming after. Coming up. Taking over.

While each generation has its challenges, these "30-something and below" men and women will never be able to fully understand the darkness we lived with during the 1960s and early 1970s. They will never know about having to hide under their desks at school because we were practicing our defensive maneuvers for the ultimate war with Russia when they would drop an atomic bomb on us (as if hiding under our chairs would help). However, in all fairness, the emergents have had their Columbine and Virginia Tech. They still hide under their chairs—just for a different reason.

They won't have to feel the horrible angst that was felt in the 1960s because of the social revolution that was taking place in America—the race riots, the assassination of President Kennedy, his brother Robert, and Martin Luther King Jr. They will never comprehend the national tremors that were created by the incredibly unpopular war in Vietnam. As a teenager, I remember lying in front of the television night after night watching the news showing the black body bags with dead soldiers in them, hearing how many had been killed that day and what the total number was, night after night after night. You felt like you were living in a bad dream from which you were never going to wake up. Over 50,000 Americans died in that war. It was a horribly depressing time in America. The entire country was in anguish as we seemed mired in social upheaval, political scandals, and international mayhem.

Depending on how you perceive it, these young adults are either the victims or the beneficiaries of the sexual revolution that happened in the '60s as well. A popular placard at anti-war demonstrations was "Make Love, Not War." It reflected the rapidly changing moral values our country was experiencing. But the decline of being in a committed relationship and the liberating free love movement brought sex out of the bedroom and into our living rooms, kitchens, airplane bathrooms, television, movies, billboards, and everywhere else you cared to look.

They won't know much about the Carter years, when the national speed limit was dropped to fifty-five (because of an oil shortage) and the President in essence cancelled Christmas one year by requesting that all Americans not put Christmas lights on their homes because of the wasted energy consumption. By the way, do you have any idea how long it takes to drive through Kansas at fifty-five mph?

But one of the key reasons I envy people in their teens, twenties, and thirties is because of the vast amount of information that is now available concerning the subject of homosexuality. I'm not saying that it's all legitimate information, but there is a lot being written about it today.

When I was a teenager in the 1960s there was *very* little written about the subject. That was still at a point in time when homosexuality was considered a mental illness by the American Psychiatric Association. In the DSM (The Diagnostic and Statistical Manual of mental disorders) that's what it was—a mental disorder. As you are probably aware, there are still some today who put it in that category.

I remember, because of my shame and embarrassment, sneaking into the public library, going to the card catalog (another thing many emergents today might be totally unfamiliar with), finding the section that had books on human sexuality, and looking in vain for anything that would help me understand the feelings I was living with. Except for a few brief paragraphs here and there which all seemed to end with the idea that homosexuality was a horrible abnormality, there was nothing. It was like dipping into a well and bringing up a bucketful of sand.

I think it's important right now that I be as honest with you as I can without being graphic or a sensationalist. I was raised in a very moral home. I suppose it would be fair to say that most kids were raised in somewhat moral homes back in the 1950s and early 1960s. But a defining moment came for me when I was probably about fifteen or so. One Sunday afternoon my dad asked me to go for a ride in the car with him. That's not something we'd ever done before so I knew something was up. Well, it was time for "the talk." The birds and the bees talk. You know. The "where do babies come from" discussion.

I already knew about that, but what I wasn't prepared for was the strong feelings my dad had about homosexuals. Now I want you to know that I love my father and do not want to dishonor him in any way, but I still need to share what he said. There was a lot of ranting and raving that went on that Sunday afternoon on the part of my dad. He made it very clear how he felt about "fags," "homos," and "queers," and what he would do if one ever tried to put a move on him. And as I was sitting in the passenger seat taking all this in, the one thought that kept going over and over in my mind was, "Dad, that's *me* you're talking about. Is that how you would feel about *me* if you knew my secret?"

I don't know if there are degrees of death, but if there are it was in that moment, on that Sunday afternoon, that I died a little more. I suddenly felt more alone than I had ever felt in my life. Because now, in addition to knowing how society in general viewed homosexuality, I also knew how the man I loved most in the world felt about it as well. I felt like a batter who had just had *strike two* called against him.

For a while during high school I worked at a gas station. This was in the days before self-service stations, so whenever a car came in it was immediately surrounded by three or four attendants who would wash the windows, check the oil, fill it with gas, check all the tires, vacuum the inside, and do anything else the customer might want done. And this was all done for about twenty-five cents a gallon! In fact, I remember during one gas war our gas went down to nineteen cents a gallon (I'm not kidding). We had cars lined up for what seemed liked forever and on each and every car we had to go through the entire procedure. Just in case any of you are wondering, *that's* what is meant by good "old-fashioned" customer service.

It was at the gas station however that I met my first two gay guys. They were two young men in their early twenties who worked as mechanics at the station. Both of them were farm boys from Nebraska. They'd moved to the big city and were living together in a day and age when that was a rarity. They were also very straight-acting gay men. There was nothing effeminate about them. Grease under the fingernails. Sports nuts. Masculine looking. And both of them were genuinely nice guys.

At one point, I needed some brakes on my car and they offered to do the work for me on a Saturday over at their apartment. I arrived about 8:00 that morning and walked into the living room, to find a mattress in the middle of the floor. I asked the guy who let me in what the mattress was doing there and he said he'd slept there.

I asked him if that was where he always slept (since it was a one bedroom apartment) and he said no, but his roommate had had a "friend" sleep over for the night. Then moments later two men come walking out of the bedroom. I'd known these guys for a number of months but that was the first indication I had that they played for a different team.

That realization did a couple of things for me. First of all it intrigued me immensely. How in the world did those two guys ever make the journey (not physical but in every other way) from the farmlands of Nebraska to one of the ultimate indicators of being out—that of living together? And second, for the first time in my life I realized that there were at least two other people who obviously had feelings like I had, and in some strange way, that was comforting to me. I didn't feel so all alone.

I never talked with them about their story—in fact I never asked them anything about their lifestyle. I wish now that I had, but I never got up enough courage to do that. I also never let them into my secret world. I was too embarrassed and ashamed to do that as well. Consequently I stayed very much alone, but with a growing awareness that there were others who were grappling with their sexual identity. I've often thought about those two young men over the years and wonder what happened to them. I hope they're still alive.

Oh, there's one last thing I envy about people born in the 1970s, 1980s and 1990s. They won't ever have to experience the fashion faux pas of the century—polyester leisure suits, of which I had two—one bright blue and the other a putrid lime green. Thank goodness some things go out of style, go into the closet, and stay there. Some other things however, come out of the closet and are here to stay.

REFLECTION #1

EVANGELICALS

I've recently had a couple of enjoyable evenings with a Jewish man. Our first conversation became deep, very fast. He was aware of my situation, and he himself has a daughter who is a lesbian living with another woman. This gentleman is very successful in the academic world, and quite intelligent and thoughtful. Frankly, I appreciated his straight-forward honesty and questions. It makes you feel a whole lot closer to an individual (and in this case very much understood) when you can get past the weather and the job and all that other shallow stuff that seems to occupy so much of our conversations with others.

The second time we got together he was intrigued by the term, evangelical. He also wanted to know what born again meant. We hadn't been discussing these ideas—he brought them up on his own. Over the years, he'd heard the terms tossed around and was curious. He was genuinely interested in my explaining these concepts.

Today, everybody in our society has an impression of these two words. For some, the mere mention of evangelical or born again is enough to elicit mockery and disdain. It's important for me that we seek to understand these expressions because within the gay community these terms are associated with people who are deemed to be the enemy. It is the evangelical Christian right and the born again Christians who evidence the most hostility towards gay men and women. That bothers me a lot.

Let me see if I can bring some clarity to these concepts. In this Reflection I want to talk about the word, evangelical. Definitions can be very fluid, but generally I'll be giving some accurate descriptions. In the Christian world, as in any faith system, there is a spectrum of beliefs ranging from ultra-liberal to ultra-conservative.

In the ultra-liberal range are churches where members may never open up a Bible. The pastor may or may not preach a sermon that is based in the Bible. It might be nothing more than a ten minute commentary on a social ill of the day. Many ultra-liberals do not even believe much of the Bible. They are intently focused on social issues, which by the way, *is* a key component to the Christian message. I'm really going to step into alligator-filled waters now, but many of the ultra-liberal Christians are Democrats. These are scary people in my book. Not because they are Democrats but because they are ignoring a vital aspect of the Christian faith: there's not a lot of encouragement to develop a personal, one-on-one, life-changing relationship with God. So they are "Christian" and while their faith may move them to embrace and work for social causes like global warming, civil rights issues, the poor, the disenfranchised of society, health care, or the world-wide AIDS crisis, their faith may not touch their personal spirit. They may or may not work at trying to develop a personal relationship with God and so their belief might be more cause-driven rather than heart-centered.

At the opposite end of this extreme are the ultra-conservatives. These people can be scary as well. I have a friend who was working on a project for one of his seminary classes for which he was required to interview a few pastors. One of the men he picked was an ultra-conservative. When they went out for coffee one of the first things this pastor said was, "I want you to know, I'm a separatist." In other words, he and his followers were committed to remaining distant from people not "like them," uninvolved with the messiness of people's lives and generally going through this life living in a make believe la-la land.

Ultra-conservatives come from a handful of very strict, fundamental colleges and seminaries around the country. They often believe there is only one correct version of the Bible—the King James Version. They have a whole lot of rules and regulations that they live by—trying to keep themselves boxed in and closed off from the world. My observation of these people is that they are not very winsome. They really aren't much fun to be around. But to them, life isn't about having fun. Politically, they would more than likely be Republicans. The reason they are scary people to me isn't because they are Republicans, but because they also are ignoring a vital aspect of the Christian faith: they don't seem to be concerned about many of the social causes in which true followers of Christ should be investing some energy and resources, things like global warming, civil rights issues, the poor, the disenfranchised of society, health care, and the world-wide AIDS crisis—those very things the liberal Christians are concerned about.

So you have ultra-liberal on one end and ultra-conservative at the other. The evangelicals would fall somewhere to the right of center, closer to the ultra-conservatives than to the ultra-liberals. But it would be a mistake to put evangelicals in the same camp as the ultra-conservatives. The word evangelical, is a sister word to evangelism. Evangelism is simply sharing with other people what you believe about God and faith and Jesus Christ. It's a key part of the Christian message. One of the last things Jesus told his disciples is recorded in Matthew 28: "All authority in heaven and on earth has been given to me. Therefore go and make disciples of all nations, baptizing them in the name of the Father and of the Son and of the Holy Spirit, and teaching them to obey everything I have commanded you. And surely I am with you always, to the very end of the age."[5]

This is called the Great Commission. Go and make disciples. As we travel through our world we are to be sharing with people the good news of God—that Jesus

Christ loves them and has made it possible for them to have a relationship with the Creator God who made them. That's evangelism. Evangelicals are people who take that calling seriously and are seeking to share that good news. Sadly however, we've often shared some really *good* news in some really *bad* ways.

In addition, there are other key distinctions concerning evangelicals.

They believe that the Bible is God's Word. That is to say, evangelicals believe that the content in the Bible is true and accurate. They believe God actually helped the writers of the Bible pen what He wanted them to say, so that it really is more than just a collection of human authors writing down their own ideas and thoughts. The Bible is God's love letter to us, accurate and without error. By the way, before that idea is dismissed as being antiquated ignorance and possibly even arrogance, you might want to spend some time researching the whole topic. There is a lot of very convincing evidence that supports such a position.

However, it is this belief in the truthfulness of the Bible that becomes the focal point of an enormous amount of tension for people like me and many others. The reason for this is that there are a lot of things in the Bible that are hard to understand. There are seemingly contradictory passages, some things don't ring true with our human experience, and other things seem to suggest ideas that culturally we struggle with today. Having said that, there comes a point in time when a thinking individual needs to do honest, thorough research on what the Bible actually is, how it came to be, why it can be considered trustworthy, and then employ the mystical dynamic that is so often missing from the lives of many—*faith*. Somewhere along the line faith has to come into play, and by faith you begin accepting some things that you cannot explain simply by human reasoning.

Also, because of their belief in the Great Commission, evangelicals would emphasize the importance of personally encountering a living God. The thought is this: if God is who He is presented to be in the Bible, then He is a God who created us, loves us intensely, and desperately wants to be in a relationship with us. Since He is real and He is a person, He can be known just like any other person. The way an individual gets to know God is vitally connected to the person and work of Jesus Christ, whom the Christian world believes was God coming to earth in human form and flesh. While Jesus is truly the cornerstone of the Christian Church, He becomes extremely important to evangelicals—not just as an historical figure or a great example of how to live our lives, but as a living person who can be known and related to—today, right here, right now.

Finally, it is because of the truth that you can relate to God in a personal way through the person of Jesus, that evangelicals have an emphasis on the conversion experience. This conversion experience is also called being "saved" or the "new birth" or being "born again," which is a term Jesus used in John 3:3. That's why evangelicals are sometimes referred to as born again Christians.

Before we leave this topic of evangelicals, I want to address one other thing. As I alluded to earlier, sadly the term "evangelical" means one thing to those within the movement and something entirely different to the general public. There is a part of me that actually hates being called an evangelical (even though that's what I am) because in today's society it has such a negative connotation. The term has been wed and has gotten into bed with right-wing Republican politics and has also become connected to a handful of moral issues that our society is dealing with right now: abortion, gay-rights, the breakdown of the family, capital punishment, the war in Iraq. Republican platforms aside, it's important we recognize that *none* of these issues are really at the heart of evangelical belief, but tragically those issues are identifying evangelicals today.

I'm not even sure I want to consider myself part of the evangelical movement anymore, because the term is conveying information to people that I personally don't want to suggest. That's not necessarily a bad thing because when people lose the convenience of a label to identify themselves, it forces them to be prepared to be more specific about what they actually believe.

That's a good thing. Sometimes, a label can be nothing more than a wall to hide behind for people who don't want to really invest some brain cells in thinking through challenging issues.

Fundamentally, I wish we didn't make things so complicated. We're compulsive about labeling people, so that we know who to stay away from and who to attach ourselves to. I don't like that. Labeling people seems to go against everything Jesus taught us. He said that the two greatest commandments were to "…love the Lord your God with all your heart, all your soul and all your strength and all your mind and love your neighbor as yourself."[6] *Love God* and *love people.* To me, *this* is the essence of the Christian faith. Anything beyond that is man's attempt to classify. Anything beyond that is man's attempt to divide, distinguish, separate, categorize, box in, keep out, welcome some, and disregard others. Thus we have over 9,000 different Christian denominations in the world today *all* claiming to have the inside track on the truth of God.

If I'm going to be labeled, a big part of me would like to just be identified as a *LGLP* Christian. It would be nice if people could look at me and see that that I'm simply seeking to love God and love people. Period.

At least it's a noble goal to strive for.

---

[5] Matthew 28:18-20
[6] Luke 10:27

REFLECTION #2

BORN AGAIN

Since my Jewish friend was also interested in the term "born again" let me reflect on that idea as well.

It's interesting how people in our society seem to have this phrase roll off their tongue with a certain sense of disgust, disdain, and amusement. Born again Christians are not very popular in our society at the moment. In part it's because we have allowed ourselves to be attached to social and political issues that we really have no business being associated with. When the *issues* that we become identified with overshadow the *message* we should be sharing, we should realize that something has gone horribly wrong.

This term, born again is one Jesus used. John 3 reads as follows [Italics mine]: "Now there was a man of the Pharisees named Nicodemus, a member of the Jewish ruling council. He came to Jesus at night and said, 'Rabbi, we know you are a teacher who has come from God. For no one could perform the miraculous signs you are doing if God were not with him.' In reply Jesus declared, 'I tell you the truth, no one can see the kingdom of God unless he is *born again*.' 'How can a man be born when he is old?' Nicodemus asked. 'Surely he cannot enter a second time into his mother's womb to be born!' Jesus answered, 'I tell you the truth, no one can enter the kingdom of God unless he is born of water and the Spirit. Flesh gives birth to flesh, but the Spirit gives birth to spirit. You should not be surprised at my saying, *'You must be born again.'* The wind blows wherever it pleases. You hear its sound, but you cannot tell where it comes from or where it is going. So it is with everyone born of the Spirit.' 'How can this be?' Nicodemus asked. 'You are Israel's teacher,' said Jesus, 'and do you not understand these things? I tell you the truth, we speak of what we know, and we testify to what we have seen, but still you people do not accept our testimony. I have spoken to you of earthly things and you do not believe; how then will you believe if I speak of heavenly things? No one has ever gone into heaven except the one who came from heaven—the Son of Man. Just as Moses lifted up the snake in the desert, so the Son of Man must be lifted up, that everyone who believes in him may have eternal life. For God so loved the world that he gave his one and only Son, that whoever believes in him shall not perish but have eternal life. For God did not send his Son into the world to condemn the world, but to save the world through him.'"[7]

This is a significant dialogue that occurs between these two men. Jesus tells Nicodemus that he has to be born again. It was very difficult for this old man to understand how he could crawl back into his mother's womb and be born a second time. But Jesus wasn't talking about a second physical birth. He was talking about a spiritual birth. Just as people are born of the flesh ("born of water" is the way Jesus put it), people also need to be born again, only this time "born of the Spirit." One is earthly in its origin, the other is from above. It's something God does for us when we believe in Jesus Christ ("….everyone who believes in him [Jesus] may have eternal life.") Then you have one of the most famous verses in the Bible. If you ever went to Sunday School I have no doubt that one of the first Bible verses you learned was John 3:16 "For God so loved the world that he gave his one and only Son, that whoever believes in him shall not perish but have eternal life." That's a great verse. But so also is the one that comes right after it—verse 17: "For God did not send his Son into the world to condemn the world, but to save the world through him."

Being born again means that individuals believe that God sent Jesus into the world in order for each of us to be able to experience eternal life. Born again Christians are people who have personally accepted that truth and believe by faith that Jesus will bring them into God's presence when they die.

It's a simple idea, yet incredibly profound. When a person comes to that point of acceptance, literally his or her whole life begins to change. It's a spiritual thing. That's what happened to me when I was seventeen. Up until that time in my life I never really had anyone explain to me that God loved me so much that He sent His Son into this world to come and get me. My grandmother was the one that shared that truth with me.

The memories I have of my grandmother are very warm ones. She and Grandpa never really had a lot in the way of this world's stuff. He worked as a barber in a little shop on their farm just a few miles outside a small Missouri town. Grandma sold Avon. They were staunch Southern Baptists and if my dad is to be believed, Grandpa was asked to leave more than one Baptist church because he kept getting into arguments with the preacher—during the services. Grandpa was definitely an opinionated man.

The thing I remember most about my grandmother was her singing. She had a beautiful voice and she was constantly singing hymns. She'd be in the kitchen cooking up donuts, biscuits and gravy for breakfast, cleaning the house, or canning green beans from her garden and she'd be singing. She always seemed to have a song in her heart. That was made even more interesting to me because they were extremely poor people and Grandpa wasn't the easiest person to live with.

In fact his kids would all say that I'm being way too easy on him. He could be downright mean and abusive. As a child, my dad was locked in the coal cellar for punishment, horsewhipped many times, and even at the age of twenty-one, as a married man, Grandpa slapped him so hard for lighting up a cigarette in the house that it knocked Dad out of his chair. Not having much materially and living with an abusive husband could make a lot of women very depressed. Grandma had a very hard life. What did she have to sing about? Her song came from her love for God. He put something in her spirit, in her soul, that transcended her earthly circumstances.

I remember when we would visit how often I would see her reading her Bible. She loved the Bible. And she knew it. She knew a lot of it. The interesting thing was Grandma never got past the eighth grade in school. She wasn't book taught but she was Book taught. She had a lot of spiritual wisdom that God gave her because she spent so much time reading the Bible. Over the last five years of Grandma's life she was afflicted with Alzheimer's. She gradually began to lose her grip on reality, sinking further and further into that world from which there is no return. This is the world that Nancy Reagan called "the long goodbye" as her husband Ronald drifted away.

Grandma finally even lost the ability to remember the names of her own children, or who her husband was. Alzheimer's is a horrible disease. My wife's mother also had it before she died. We've seen it up close and personal and it's a challenging time for family members. But the thing about Grandma's last few years was this: even though she had literally lost her mind, she could still sing beautifully. She couldn't put a sentence together, but when she started singing, she could sing an entire hymn and not miss a word. She couldn't remember the names of her children but she could quote passages from the Bible. It was amazing. It showed me that there is a deeper part of the human being that goes beyond the mind. It's the spirit, the place where God comes and communicates with us.

I am forever grateful to my grandmother. Because it was while I was visiting Grandma and Grandpa at the farm one summer that she shared God's love for me through Jesus Christ. I accepted that love. I was seventeen and my life would never be the same. Grandma shared with me a truth that profoundly changed my life.

However, placing my faith in Jesus Christ, and embracing the teachings of the Bible also became profoundly disturbing.

---

[7] John 3:1-17

 FOUR

A DOUBLE-EDGED SWORD

EVERY SILVER LINING has a cloud. That's not a misprint. How is it that something so exciting, so good, so life-changing can also be the very thing that causes a person huge distress? When I experienced my conversion, I fell in love. I realized that Jesus Christ loved me and I determined to make it my aim in life to serve Him and try to honor Him out of a grateful heart.

I started off my Christian experience full of joy and excited anticipation. I quickly got involved in a church, began attending a dynamic college group, started growing spiritually by leaps and bounds, and was having a great time. I also started reading the Bible voraciously, and that's when my trouble began. It didn't take me long to discover that there were some passages in the Bible that spoke to the issue of homosexuality. They weren't very positive comments either. That's when my silver lining started developing its cloud.

When I think back on it, deep down inside I thought, hoped, and prayed that becoming a Christian would "cure" me. That my conversion, as profound and significant as it was, would affect this deep part of my life and that maybe God would change me. At least that's how I began to pray because I had no doubt about God's ability to do above and beyond anything that I could ever think about or ask Him for. I didn't doubt it then and I don't doubt it now. However, that's been almost 40 years ago, and my struggle hasn't gotten any easier.

There are basically six passages in the Bible that speak to the issue of homosexuality either directly or indirectly.

Genesis 1-2 (Creation Account)

The first two chapters of the Bible deal with creation. The only reason these chapters would need to be included in a discussion of homosexuality is because in Genesis 2 it states that in creating humankind, God made humankind male and female. Then it goes on to say, "But for Adam no suitable helper was found. So the LORD God caused the man to fall into a deep sleep, and while he was sleeping, he took one of the man's ribs and closed up the place with flesh. Then the LORD God made a woman from the rib he had taken out of the man and he brought her to the man. The man said, 'This is now bone of my bones and flesh of my flesh; she shall be called 'woman,' for she was taken out of man.' For this reason a man will leave his father and mother and be united to his wife, and they will become one flesh. The man and his wife were both naked, and they felt no shame."[8]

In the opening pages of the Bible there is the implied idea that men and women are to be together. Or as some Christians, thinking they're being cute, like to say: "It was Adam and Eve, not Adam and Steve." People shouldn't trivialize such a serious issue.

Genesis 19 (Sodom Account)

The biblical account of Sodom and Gomorrah is often referenced in considering the issue of homosexuality. I'm going to spend some time on this section because there are things that need to be addressed.

> "The two angels arrived at Sodom in the evening, and Lot was sitting in the gateway of the city. When he saw them, he got up to meet them and bowed down with his face to the ground. 'My lords,' he said, 'please turn aside to your servant's house. You can wash your feet and spend the night and then go on your way early in the morning.' 'No,' they answered, 'we will spend the night in the square.' But he

insisted so strongly that they did go with him and entered his house. He prepared a meal for them, baking bread without yeast, and they ate. Before they had gone to bed, all the men from every part of the city of Sodom—both young and old—surrounded the house. They called to Lot, 'Where are the men who came to you tonight? Bring them out to us so that we can have sex with them.' Lot went outside to meet them and shut the door behind him and said, 'No, my friends. Don't do this wicked thing. Look, I have two daughters who have never slept with a man. Let me bring them out to you, and you can do what you like with them. But don't do anything to these men, for they have come under the protection of my roof.' 'Get out of our way,' they replied. And they said, 'This fellow came here as an alien, and now he wants to play the judge! We'll treat you worse than them.' They kept bringing pressure on Lot and moved forward to break down the door. But the men inside reached out and pulled Lot back into the house and shut the door. Then they struck the men who were at the door of the house, young and old, with blindness so that they could not find the door."[9]

This is a very interesting section of scripture. I'm hesitant however, to put much stock in it one way or the other, because it's not as cut and dried as one might think through a just casual reading of the passage. Unfortunately, these verses have taken on a central role in the study of homosexuality. It's important that we understand the context of this account. God sends two angels to warn Abraham's nephew, Lot, about the impending destruction of Sodom. If we stop here for a moment we will see that even before sending the angels, God intended to destroy Sodom. So, whatever the reason for the city's destruction, it had to do with the sin of Sodom before this event.

However, it's fascinating to me that the very phrase "the sin of sodomy" has come to refer to same-sex relations. That seems to be the primary thing people focus on when they address this passage. For example, very little is said about the wickedness and utter depravity of Lot in offering his own daughters to these men in lieu of the guests in his home. To me, *that's* perverse. In our culture today, it makes no sense to us that hospitality was an almost sacred concept in biblical times, so much so that you would be willing to give your daughters over to a group of men to be violently raped rather than have the guests in your home dishonored. But that's the distinction Lot expresses: the visitors are his guests, so please don't harm them. Regardless, what is happening here in this story is a form of rape. The crowd of men wanted to brutally and sadistically sexually assault these angels, as they would have done with Lot's daughters if the story had progressed further.

It is also interesting in that we are specifically told in another portion of scripture *why* God destroyed the city of Sodom. "Sodom's sins were pride, gluttony, and laziness, while the poor and needy suffered outside her door."[10] The New International Version renders it this way: "Now this was the sin of your sister Sodom: She and her daughters were arrogant, overfed and unconcerned; they did not help the poor and needy. They were haughty and did detestable things before me. Therefore I did away with them…"[11] The detestable things, the things God got angry about, were their arrogant pride, their self-indulgence, and their lack of compassion for the poor and needy.

In the New Testament we have one verse that focuses on the sexual issue more specifically. "In a similar way, Sodom and Gomorrah and the surrounding towns gave themselves up to sexual immorality and perversion. They serve as an example of those who suffer the punishment of eternal fire."[12]

If we take both the Ezekiel and the Jude passage together, it would seem that there were *multiple* reasons that caused God to destroy the city of Sodom. My caution here is that we need to be careful about singling out one particular issue and emphasizing it more than all the others.

Leviticus 18 and 20 (Holiness Code)

"Do not lie with a man as one lies with a woman; that is detestable."[13]

"If a man lies with a man as one lies with a woman, both of them have done what is detestable. They must be put to death; their blood will be on their own heads."[14]

Again, a casual reading of these verses does not reveal the difficulty with them. Moses (the writer of Leviticus) could have said, "If a man lies with a man, both of them have done what is detestable." It would have been very clear as to what Moses meant because the term, "lie" is known to be the Old Testament word for having sexual relations.

Why did he include the qualifying phrase, "as one lies with a woman" in both of these passages? It's redundant and unnecessary. However, having a cultural understanding of the dominant role of the male and the subservient role of the female in Old Testament Jewish society causes us to realize that there is something else going on here other than just two men having sexual relations. It's also interesting to note that there is no corresponding command for woman. We are told that women should not have sex with animals,[15] but there is nothing in the entire Old Testament about women having sexual relations with other women. Is it O.K. for women but not for men? What's going on here?

These two verses are part of what's known as the Holiness Code, and to get into a discussion of that Code is outside the intent of this book. But here is the relevant point: there are over 600 laws in the Old Testament and the book of Leviticus contains many of those laws. The Holiness Code was given to protect the Israelites from idolatry and to distinguish them from the pagan cultures that surrounded them. Leviticus 18 begins, "And the Lord said to Moses, 'Say to the people of Israel, I am the Lord your God. You shall not do as they do in the land of Egypt, where you dwelt, and you shall not do as they do in the land of Canaan, to which I am bringing you. You shall not walk in their statutes. You shall do my ordinances and keep my statutes and walk in them. I am the Lord your God…'"[16]

These 600-plus laws cover a lot of interesting territory, containing commandments for men not to shave the edges of their beards;[17] orders not to have intercourse with a woman during menstruation;[18] not to sow different crops in the same field;[19] the death penalty is prescribed for people who work on the Sabbath;[20] as well as for cursing;[21] in addition there are numerous dietary laws; the command not to put tattoos on your body; the instruction to stone psychics and put adulterers to death; how to handle mildew; what to do with infectious skin diseases; how to purify a woman after childbirth, and a whole host of other very fascinating regulations, most of which are not followed today.

At some point there has to be an honest evaluation of the above two verses and how they fit in with the rest of the Holiness Code, and if all of these laws within the Code are relevant today. The difficulty lies in just how we interpret this Code. All of this points to the necessity of interpreting scriptural commands within the cultural context of the times they were written in, so that we are able to comprehend the meaning the authors actually intended for their writings. That could be a book in itself.[22]

Romans 1 (Letter of Paul)

"Therefore God gave them over in the sinful desires of their hearts to sexual impurity for the degrading of their bodies with one another. They exchanged the truth of God for a lie, and worshiped and served created things rather than the Creator—who is forever praised. Amen. Because of this, God gave them over to shameful lusts. Even their women exchanged natural relations for unnatural ones. In the same way the men also abandoned natural relations with women and were inflamed with lust for one another. Men committed indecent acts with other men, and received in themselves the due penalty for their perversion."[23]

After almost forty years of studying the Bible, these verses give me the greatest difficulty. With the other passages that I've listed here, there is enough obscurity within the passages themselves, the context, and the culture in which they were written to create some space for healthy, honest dialogue, and evaluation. This passage in Romans however, seems quite clear.

I Corinthians 6 (Letter of Paul)

"Do you not know that the wicked will not inherit the kingdom of God? Do not be deceived: Neither the sexually immoral nor idolaters nor adulterers nor male prostitutes nor homosexual offenders nor thieves nor the greedy nor drunkards nor slanderers nor swindlers will inherit the kingdom of God."[24]

My comment on this passage is to encourage you to notice that *along with* male prostitutes and homosexual offenders, Paul also includes a wide variety of other groups of people that many today conveniently ignore:

- those who are generally sexually immoral (people who have sex before marriage, view pornography, have lustful thoughts, visit female prostitutes, etc.)

- those who are idolaters (people who put anything or anyone above God in their life)

- adulterers (married people who have sex outside of their marriage)
- greedy people (folks who love money)
- people who get drunk (self-explanatory)
- people who slander others (folks who defame the reputation or character of another)
- swindlers (people who defraud others out of their money)

I direct the following comment to my fellow Christ-followers: We need to be consistent. If we're going to speak out with vitriolic condemnation towards those who are homosexual offenders, we'd better begin speaking out with the same acerbic passion and intensity towards all these other groups. If not, we would do well to tone down the rhetoric, because if we don't, *we* are the hypocrites.

I Timothy 1 (Letter of Paul)

"We know that the law is good if one uses it properly. We also know that law is made not for the righteous but for lawbreakers and rebels, the ungodly and sinful, the unholy and irreligious; for those who kill their fathers or mothers, for murderers, for adulterers and perverts, for slave traders and liars and perjurers—and for whatever else is contrary to sound doctrine…"[25]

The word "pervert" is the word in this passage that is commonly translated homosexual. My comment here is the same as for the previous passage, only now Paul gives us *more* groups of people to include in our diatribe:

- lawbreakers
- rebels
- ungodly
- sinful
- unholy

- irreligious

- parent killers

- all other murderers

- adulterers and perverts (finally a couple of the same ones from the previous list)

- slave traders

- liars

- perjurers

These are the Bible passages that speak to the issue of homosexuality. I have to tell you, as a new, young convert to the Christian faith, these were hard passages to swallow. Each time I read them I felt like God was punching me in the stomach. Here I had made a commitment to follow Someone, making it my goal in life to live for Him, and I had this sinking realization that in addition to society hating homosexuality and my dad not caring for it much either, now I found out that God wasn't real fond of it, as well.

At least that's how I processed what I was reading. Society. *Strike one.* Family. *Strike two.* And now God. *Strike three.* With that realization, all the guilt and shame that I had lived with up to that point in time was magnified a hundred-fold. I felt more guilty and more shameful than I had ever felt in my life, because even though my goal was to not act on my impulses, I felt God was disgusted with me *regardless* of my behavior. Thus began what would turn into a lifetime of trying to figure out how, as a Christian, I was supposed to deal with this amazingly complicated issue.

---

[8] Genesis 2:20-25
[9] Genesis 19:1-11

[10] Ezekiel 16:49-50, *New Living Translation* (NLT)
[11] Ezekiel 16:49-50
[12] Jude 1:7
[13] Leviticus 18:22
[14] Leviticus 20:13
[15] Leviticus 18:23
[16] Leviticus 18:1-4
[17] Leviticus 19:27
[18] Leviticus 18:19
[19] Leviticus 19:19
[20] Exodus 35:1-2
[21] Leviticus 24:13-16
[22] For a challenging look at this issue see, *The New Testament and Homosexuality: Contextual Background for Contemporary Debate*, Robin Scroggs, Fortress Press, Copyright © 1983. While not agreeing with everything in this book, it does provide some very thought provoking insights into the subject of biblical interpretation and the role context and culture play in determining the meaning of any given passage of scripture.
[23] Romans 1:24-27
[24] I Corinthians 6:9
[25] I Timothy 1:8-10

 FIVE

HAPPINESS

I'VE OFTEN WONDERED how a baseball player feels after he's struck out. The umpire calls the third and final strike and in front of a stadium full of onlookers he has to walk back to the dugout. Even though he probably tells himself that it's just part of the game I still think he would be experiencing a breadth of emotions: frustration, anger, disappointment, humiliation, rejection (if the fans are booing him), and sadness.

My three strikes certainly made me feel that way. In fact a while back one of Char's friends said something to her that I found intriguing. She commented that whenever she would look at me she thought my eyes looked sad. It was an interesting remark because for years, whenever I'd look at a picture of myself I would think the same thing. I guess there is some truth to the statement that the eyes are the window of the soul. Her comment got me to thinking again about some concepts I'd frequently thought about over the years. Things like: Sadness. Happiness. Joy. What exactly do those words mean?

Judith Viorst has written a wonderful book entitled, *Alexander and the Terrible, Horrible, No Good, Very Bad Day*.[26] Poor Alexander. From the moment he wakes up until he goes to sleep that night, nothing goes right for him all day long and all he wants to do is move to Australia. Part of it goes like this: "I went to sleep with gum in my mouth and now there's gum in my hair and when I got out of bed this morning I tripped on the skateboard and by mistake I dropped my sweater in the sink while the water was running and I could tell it was going to be a terrible, horrible, no good, very bad day. There were lima beans for dinner and I hate limas. There was kissing on TV and I hate kissing. My bath was too hot, I got soap in my eyes, my marble went down the drain, and I had to wear my railroad-train pajamas. I hate my railroad-train pajamas. When I went to bed Nick took back the pillow he said I could keep and the Mickey Mouse night light burned out and I bit my tongue. The cat wants to sleep with Anthony, not with me. It has been a terrible, horrible, no good, very bad day."

Can you relate? All of us have had days like that. Some days are particularly worse than others. But then again, some days seem to be particularly better than most. Once in a while I'll wake up in the morning and the minute I get out of bed I can tell it's going to be a wonderful, pleasant, good, *very* good day. It's really hard to describe. It's something I sense intuitively. But as I go through the day I notice that my spirit is lighter. I feel good, not just physically but emotionally. The world seems more alive; colors are brighter, sounds are crisper, the air has a certain intoxicating scent to it. I'm more sensitized to what's going on around me. Life seems fuller and I feel more complete, more whole, and more *alive.* I think this might be a glimpse of what heaven is going to be like.

Attempting to put some definition around my inner world of emotions can be challenging. Maybe you've experienced what I'm talking about. But, here's the thing. Whenever I have a day like that, I find myself thinking "Is this happiness? Is this what most people feel most of the time?" If it is, then I have to tell you, happiness has been a very elusive experience for me. Years ago I started keeping track of these "wonderful, pleasant, very good days" and I began to realize that in all these years of living, I can count on one hand the number of times I've felt this way. Maybe that's why someone sees sadness in my eyes.

Happiness frustrates me, probably because I've never felt I could quite get my hands around it. What exactly is it? How do we capture its essence? How do we know when we've got it? The dictionary has some interesting definitions:

> **"hap·py"** (adjective) 1. Feeling pleasure: feeling or showing pleasure, contentment or joy 2. Causing pleasure: causing or characterized by pleasure, contentment or joy 3. Satisfied: feeling satisfied that something is right or has been done right 4. Fortunate: resulting unexpectedly in something pleasant or welcome.

Yet, dictionary definitions frustrate me. The words they use to describe a word are often just as unclear as the word they are trying to define. So now I'm frustrated by happiness and I'm frustrated with the way the dictionary tries to define it.

Then there is joy. Is there a difference between joy and happiness or are they just different words for the same elusive concept? After thinking about this for a long time, I've come to a conclusion—they are different. My definitions for happiness and joy are as follows:

> Happiness: "A settled contentedness with ourselves."

> Joy: "A settled contentedness with God."

I'm not sure if "contentedness" is even a word but it's the best one I can come up with to describe what I'm talking about. Contentment is a feeling of being satisfied and at rest. It was Aristotle who said "Happiness depends on ourselves." Here is where I can get into trouble with some of my fellow Christ-followers. I agree with Aristotle. I used to think that happiness came from our relationship with God. In other words, we would say, "Happiness depends on God." I'm not sure that's correct. Rather, happiness is something that comes from within us. It is something we experience when we are able to be at rest or at peace with ourselves. I think the only way that can happen is when we are able to be comfortable in our own skin.

How can a person possibly be satisfied (content, happy) if fundamentally, they have trouble liking themselves and are not able to be the same on the outside as they are on the inside? I don't think they can. This is what has helped me understand my life better. One of the reasons for my sadness is that my outside world and my inside world have been at odds with each other and I've had trouble liking me, for *me.*

As a Christian, as a pastor, and as a married man, I've lived my life attempting to function in ways that would be healthy reflections of those roles and responsibilities. Yet all the while I've had this intense struggle on the inside with my sexuality which squarely collides with all three of those undertakings. So I've lived my life with a horrible dichotomy. I've felt one way on the inside yet thought, believed, and acted a different way on the outside. That's not a recipe for happiness—it's a set up for sadness. The more we are able to have the inside and the outside in harmony with each other, the happier we will be. That's why I define happiness as a settled contentedness with ourselves.

Joy is similar but it is rooted in a higher Person. It is something that has a strong spiritual origin. "The *joy* of the LORD is our strength."[27] Joy is something we experience when we are in relationship with God. When I know I'm right with Him and I'm in a settled, contented relationship with Him, then I experience joy. But this is why I do believe it's possible for a person to experience joy but not happiness. I *can* be in a settled, contented relationship with God and not be in that kind of relationship with myself.

Unfortunately, "being true to yourself" can be a great catch phrase for anyone who basically wants to say, "Let me live my life as I choose." In fact, even when I say "be true to yourself," part of me cringes inside. I've had people say that to me. "You have to be true to yourself, otherwise you'll never be happy." What I think they mean when they say that is that I should just admit that I'm gay, face the ramifications of that admission, deal with the fallout, and then get on with living my life. When someone says that however, I get a check in my spirit that says, "Wait a minute, your definition of being true to yourself and mine are quite different."

Jesus gave us a lot of great principles on how to live life effectively and successfully from God's point of view. He said, "…whoever wants to save his life will lose it and whoever loses his life for me will find it."[28] And also, "…whoever wants to become great among you must be your servant."[29] In other words, one of the principles for successful living *is* to focus on others—to give ourselves away in service to others. The opposite of that kind of lifestyle is to *live for yourself.* But living for yourself is *not* the same thing as *being true to yourself.* Living for yourself is a recipe for ultimate discontent because it's a very selfish way to live. Selfishness is not one of the virtues that a person can have and be genuinely happy.

A great inner transformation takes place when a person begins to live his or her life based on the premise that life is not just about them. To get our eyes off of ourselves and start being concerned about people around us and begin to give ourselves away in sacrifice and service for others—*that's* real freedom. Living that way brings a great deal of joy into a person's life.

It's been popular in Christian circles to talk about joy by saying, "Jesus, Others, and You." JOY. Focus on Jesus, put others ahead of yourself and you'll be a person of joy. While that may seem kind of cutesy, there is a real element of truth in it. As I mentioned earlier, Jesus said that the two greatest commandments were to love God and love others. He had a way of making complex things so simple. I wonder why it is that His followers seem to have a way of making simple things so complex.

We have a friend who will frequently say, "I like myself." This person is one of the cheeriest, most loved and loving, "live-life-to-the-fullest" individuals you could ever possibly hope to meet. She's a delight to be around. She's always finding new restaurants to try, new parts of town to venture in to, new stores to shop in, new experiences to experience. If you were to ask Betty if she's happy, she'd say yes. If you were to ask her why, she'd say, "Because I like myself." *That's* what I mean when I say happiness is a settled contentedness with ourselves. Part of our journey through life is getting to the point where we can all say, "I like myself. Even if there are parts of me that are uncomfortable and challenging, I still like myself." That is a very significant part of my journey right now. That is where I ultimately want to be—comfortable in my own skin—because the struggle with my sexuality has kept me *not* liking myself for so long.

For years my dad has had a way of saying goodbye. He closes his right hand to make a loose fist, then gently taps his chest and says, "Happy heart." Happy heart. I wonder if maybe he's seen the sadness that I've been trying to hide all these years as well.

---

[26] Antheneum Books, Copyright ©1972
[27] Nehemiah 8:10
[28] Matthew 16:25
[29] Matthew 20:26

 SIX

EMBRACING YOUR LIMP

WHEN I BECAME part of the Christian community I quickly learned that there are a number of spiritual disciplines to practice which, I was told, would help me grow in my relationship with God, gain victory over sin, develop my spiritual maturity and enable me to get closer to Him. These disciplines are things such as…

regular Bible study

    prayer

        faithful church attendance

        fasting

            memorizing Scripture

            tithing

                being in a small group.

I began doing all of those things with a passion. And while I felt that they were helping me in many ways as a person, none of them was helping with my deepest struggle. I just kept struggling and kept feeling even guiltier about the fact that I did struggle. I also felt very much alone.

It wasn't long after I became a Christian and got involved in a church that I was put into a position of leadership. For some reason people thought that I had what it took to lead others. So here I was, a young Christian, thrust into leadership with individuals looking to me for guidance and answers while at the same time feeling I was the last person on earth who should be in leadership. Consequently I withdrew further into my protective shell. Leadership is a very isolating position. Leadership can become a wall that separates you from others. Leaders are put on pedestals. After all, aren't people in leadership expected to have it all together? They're not supposed to struggle. It is assumed they've grown past their struggles and achieved victory over their issues and are now able to help the less fortunate figure out how to deal with theirs.

From those early years as a new Christian, and being thrust into leadership, I began to move through the various stages of my life—going to college and getting a degree in psychology. I went on to seminary for my master's degree. I got married and had kids. Char and I struggled with finances. We started the church. The church began to grow and I dealt with all the heartaches, headaches, and joys that go with that. I experienced all the regular stuff that comes with living life, regardless of a person's profession.

All the while however, I kept after God to do something with *me*. Help me. Fix me. Take these desires away from me. There were so many nights I would crawl into bed, kiss Char goodnight, roll over onto my side and cry myself to sleep begging God to make me "normal." But it never happened. I spent time with three different counselors over the years seeking their input and help. But to no avail. People have asked me how my relationship with God was during those years and how it is now. Am I mad at Him? Have I lost my faith? Is there anger? Do I blame Him? My sincere answer to all those questions is "no." I'm not mad at Him and I haven't lost my faith. Not then. Not now. And here's why:

I learned a long time ago that God is God…

He will do whatever He pleases

with whomever He pleases

however He pleases

whenever He pleases.

The Bible says it like this: He's the potter and I'm the clay and He can do with me whatever He wants.[30] My faith, which revolutionized my life, has also been the source of some incredible depths of despair. Yet that faith has been my lifeline. Without God sustaining me, and giving me the grace and strength to get through my days, I would have given up a long time ago. Even though there have been times when I haven't felt very close to God—I know He hasn't left me. I've never said, "God, where are you?" He's been there all the time, and all these years I've been hanging onto Him. I'll talk about that more in a later chapter.

I've always envied those individuals who have had an encounter with God and are instantaneously delivered from something like alcohol, drugs, or smoking. Or maybe they are healed of a physical illness or deformity, or released from some kind of crippling emotional prison they find themselves in. God does things like that with people. I've seen it.

But if a person's faith is a mature faith, one of the things that faith has to allow for is this: *God does things like that with SOME of His people—but not with ALL of His people.* Why not? That's one of the big questions I've wrestled with over the years. And by the way, there's nothing wrong with questioning aspects of your faith or any aspect of your life for that matter. I am suspicious of people who seem to have an answer for everything. To me it means they're not very smart or they're living in denial of reality.

This is one of my questions that I don't have a complete answer for, but I think part of an answer to the question is found in an encounter Jesus had with a man who had been born blind. The story is told in John 9 and begins with an interesting question:

"As He went along, He saw a man blind from birth, His disciples asked him, 'Rabbi, who sinned, this man or his parents, that he was born blind?'"[31] It was a common assumption back then that the reason people had physical disabilities was because they were sinners. Physical infirmity was viewed as a punishment from God. That's an interesting view of God, by the way, one which is still held by some people today.

Jesus responded with a theological mind-bender for these one-track-mind disciples: "Neither this man nor his parents sinned…but this happened so that the work of God might be displayed in his life."[32] Then Jesus healed him.

The blindness allowed for the work of God (the glory of God) to be seen in this man's life. In getting healed, this man's infirmity became a beacon that the work of God was able to shine through. God was glorified from this event.

But what does that say about all the blind people in life who aren't healed, those who have their blindness for life? By blindness, I'm now speaking of anything that cripples us—physical, emotional, relational, and psychological.

For one thing, it says that God obviously deals with people in different ways. Period. And that is purely by His choice. It also says that God has different ways of having His *work* be seen through different "lenses" or lives.

Another story that has always captured my imagination is found in the Old Testament. In Genesis 32:22-32 there is the story of Jacob who spends a night wrestling with God. In this wrestling match God intentionally dislocates Jacob's hip, and Jacob begins to walk with a limp. As far as I know Jacob walked with a limp the rest of his life. It was a physical reminder to Jacob of the struggle he had with God. Through that experience Jacob's life became yet another lens through which the work of God was displayed.

In one situation, a blind man is healed by God; in another situation a man is crippled by God, yet through both lives God's work is seen. Both men had to *embrace* their encounter with God and the resulting consequences.

I want to talk about embracing our encounters—our experiences with God. God works in each of our lives in different ways. In one sense that is a very beautiful thing because it reflects the incredible creativity and diversity of God. I'll never forget the first time I strapped on a scuba tank, put on my mask and flippers, and dropped down into the turquoise waters off a Caribbean island. As I went down to about forty feet and began swimming over coral reefs, a whole new world opened up before my eyes; the rainbow colors of the coral, the amazing variety and colors of the fish, the plants, the other sea creatures from turtles to sea snakes to eels and manta rays. While I was experiencing all of this, I distinctly remember thinking, "If it weren't for the invention of the camera and the Discovery channel, this is a world that the vast majority of the human race would have no idea even exists. Yet here it is. And it is simply because of the infinite creativity of a mind-boggling God that it's all here. He made it for His glory. He takes pleasure in it." For centuries, only a small handful of the human race even knew what was down there, yet God made it—for His own enjoyment.

Whatever else you may think or say about God, He is a God of infinite, creative diversity. God loves variety. God loves uniqueness. Just look at the human race: every one of us is different. Even identical twins aren't completely identical. Billions upon billions of people and each one has the unique, creative fingerprint of God on them. One is short, the other tall. One is black, the other white. One is skinny, the other not-so-skinny. One has blue eyes, another green. The list of differences is endless.

It seems to me that there is a lot of arrogance on the part of Christian leaders when we try to "box-in" an infinite God. When we start telling people, "This is how God acts. This is what He will do. This is how He will do it. This is what you can expect and if you want to be spiritual this is how you need to relate to Him." Yes, there are certain principles that we find in the Bible that God says, if we live according to those principles our lives will be blessed. No question about that. That's not what I'm talking about. There seems to be an unpredictable, mysterious side to God's nature. He is full of surprises and apparently loves them! Is it not possible that an infinite God has an infinite variety of ways of acting towards people and working with them so that His purposes can be accomplished in their lives? I think so. Thus we all have our journeys—our individual stories which reflect how God is working in *us*.

Sadly, I think we've sold people a bill of goods as it relates to spiritual maturity and what Christian growth is supposed to look like. For some reason we have assumed and taught that spiritual maturity is to be equated with "increasingly getting our act together." That the more I get my issues under control, the more spiritual I am.

That phrase, "increasingly getting our act together" comes from a book by Dan Stone and Greg Smith entitled, *The Rest of the Gospel.* It seems most of the focus for Christians these days is on what *they* need to *do* in order to get close to God—avoid certain behaviors, places or people, attend church faithfully, give consistently, read the Bible regularly, and a variety of other spiritual practices.

That's only *part* of the Gospel story. The rest of the story involves our understanding of what God has already *done* to get close to us. When we comprehend *that* part of the Gospel and embrace it, we can actually begin to relax and start to enjoy our relationship with Him. Sadly, I haven't met too many Christians who seem to enjoy the relationship they have with the Father. For most it seems to be a relationship that weighs heavy on them. By the way, the subtitle of that book is: *When the partial Gospel has worn you out.* That's what continually *trying* to get close to God does you know—it wears you out because you are constantly working to try and do all the things that you think you need to do in order to make God happy with you. That can be a very frustrating way to live.

In a discussion about Christian growth the authors write that real Christian growth is the act of God wooing our soul back from its fascination with all the things in the outer world that capture our attention and instead developing a fascination with the inner world of life with God. I love that term "wooing." God is not a strong arm. He's more like a loving pursuer. He is calling out to us, encouraging us, drawing us to Himself by helping us focus less and less on the outer and more and more on the inner.

Consider this quote from the book: "Growing in Christ doesn't mean increasingly getting our act together, but being wooed back. God wants to woo us back in every area that our soul is turned outward. Wherever we aren't wooed back, we are vulnerable to the call of the outer—our body and its appetites, the world or Satan. Do you see what life is all about? God means to turn the whole soul slowly back to Him, to the union of His Spirit and our spirit. He isn't concerned about instant perfection. He wants steady progress in our inner knowing. Christian growth isn't striving. It's us letting the Spirit woo us back, so that we become preoccupied with Him…"[33] That's *really* good.

We set people up for failure and frustration when we teach them that they have to increasingly get their act together if they want to be spiritually mature. We actually encourage people to focus on the wrong thing. What we need to be helping people focus on isn't the weakness that they are trying (by the energy of human will power) to eradicate, but rather to turn their focus to God. God is perfectly capable of dealing with any weakness, infirmity, or habit that we may have. But the more we focus our attention on our weakness the more frustrated we will become. This is because:

> "Whatever you put your attention on will grow stronger in your life."
>
> –Deepak Chopra

It's just that simple. We're focusing on the wrong thing. We need to be able to let go of our weakness by changing our focus. Give our weakness to God by acknowledging our powerlessness to do anything about it and stop focusing so much of our time, energy and mental resources on it. There is a lot of truth found in the Serenity Prayer:

> "God grant me the serenity
> to accept the things I cannot change;
> courage to change the things I can;
> and the wisdom to know the difference.
>
>
> Living one day at a time;
> Enjoying one moment at a time;
> Accepting hardships as the pathway to peace;
> Taking, as He did, this sinful world
> as it is, not as I would have it;
> Trusting that He will make all things right
> if I surrender to His Will;
> That I may be reasonably happy in this life
> and supremely happy with Him
> Forever in the next.
> Amen."
>
> —Reinhold Niebuhr

Perhaps we can find some sense of freedom by admitting we are helpless to do anything about our weakness and instead turn our attention to letting God woo us back to Himself. Focus on becoming more preoccupied with Him.

Then, seek to *embrace* (accept, understand, welcome) how He is working in our life.

- If He chooses to treat us like the man born blind—rejoice.

- If He chooses to treat us like Jacob—rejoice.

- If He wants to take care of our issue—He will.

- If He doesn't—then embrace it.

Accept our weakness as God's unique way of dealing with us and choose to believe (and perhaps even *thrive* in the knowledge) that somehow what we are experiencing will be something through which the work of God can be seen. As we accept with grace what He gives in our life, it can become a fountain of blessing for us and others.

The apostle Paul had what he called a "thorn in the flesh." The story is told in II Corinthians 12. In that chapter Paul is talking about all the visions and revelations God gave him. He wanted to be careful not to come across as a braggart because of all that God had shown him, so he told the Corinthians about a thorn in the flesh that God gave him. "To keep me from becoming conceited because of these surpassingly great revelations, there was given me a thorn in my flesh, a messenger of Satan, to torment me. Three times I pleaded with the Lord to take it away from me. But he said to me, 'My grace is sufficient for you, for my power is made perfect in weakness.' Therefore I will boast all the more gladly about my weaknesses, so that Christ's power may rest on me. That is why, for Christ's sake, I delight in weaknesses…for when I am weak, then I am strong."[34]

We don't know what the thorn in the flesh was. Frankly, it doesn't matter. Whatever it was, Paul desperately wanted it gone from his life. But God told him to stop praying about it and embrace it *because* it was in the embracing of his thorn that the power of God would be seen more clearly in Paul's life. God promised to give grace so that Paul could endure it.

Embracing our weakness enables the strength of God to be manifest in our lives.

When we do that, genuine spiritual maturity is truly being experienced because it is *less* of us and *more* of Him. Instead of thinking that the only way we'll be spiritually mature is to increasingly get our act together, perhaps we should attempt to re-frame our lives and struggles from a different angle.

Embrace our limp.

Don't run from it.

Don't cover it up.

Stop continually begging God to change it.

Quit constantly focusing on it.

Instead...

Realize that in our weakness He is made strong.

Realize that His grace is sufficient.

And realize that our limp can actually be something that draws us close to God and through it God's work can uniquely be revealed through us.

The more I think about it, the Apostle Paul was an amazing man. It reveals a great deal about character to be able to say, "I *delight* in weakness...for when I am weak, then I am strong." That's his way of saying, "I've embraced my limp." At this point in my life, I'm seeking to embrace mine.

---

[30] Romans 9:20-21
[31] John 9:1-2
[32] John 9:3

[33] *The Rest of the Gospel*, Dan Stone and Greg Smith, One Press, Copyright © 2000, pp. 170-171

[34] II Corinthians 12:7-10

 SEVEN

THE DREAM KILLER

SHORTLY AFTER I MADE a decision to follow God at the age of seventeen, I experienced a growing sense that I was supposed to go into the ministry. This was a real shift in thinking for me because ever since junior high, I had planned on becoming a doctor—an orthopedic surgeon to be exact. I think breaking my arm three times, as well as my nose and a big toe over the years had produced that interest in me. I didn't have a clue as to what you had to do in order to become a minister, so I went to one of the pastors at the church I had begun attending, told him my situation, and asked for his advice. He had graduated from a Christian college in the Midwest and suggested I try that one. Without exploring any other college options, I applied and was accepted at his alma mater.

That fall my mom and dad took me to the small town where the school was located, dropped me off, said their goodbyes and suddenly I was a big time college student. Thus began my first exposure as a relatively new Christ-follower to something that has haunted me to this very day. In Christian circles it's called, legalism.

I don't want to put this college down. That's why I prefer to not tell you the name of the school. The fact is, it was representative of a lot of Christian colleges at the time, and for that matter there are still schools like it today. But the school had a code of ethics, a standard of behavior, and list of rules which students were expected to abide by. I willingly signed on the dotted line saying that I would adhere to their standards. The story I'm about to tell you reflects poorly on me, not the school.

As the first semester wore on, something started happening in me. I began to develop a tremendously strong desire to break all the rules I had agreed to obey. It went from the serious to the ridiculous. This was the type of school where girls had to have their dresses a certain length—they could come up no higher than about one inch above the knee, and frequently girls were called in and their dresses were measured by the dean of women. Guys couldn't have their hair hanging over their ears. This was in the 1970s when long hair was the norm, and short hair was out. I didn't like the fact that I had to have my hair short. I let my hair grow but when I went to class or a school event, I combed it in such a way that it was off my ears, as the rules stipulated.

We had a curfew every night. I think it was 10:00 on weeknights and midnight on weekends. At 10:00 and midnight the doors to the dorms would be locked. You could still get out, but you couldn't get in. If you happened to miss curfew, you had to go get a Resident Advisor to let you in and you'd get put on notice. I didn't like the fact that I had to be in by 10:00 so by the time it got to be spring of that year, some buddies and I found a way to get around that requirement. We would be in our rooms when we were supposed to, and then we'd wait a few hours and slip out, quietly drive off campus with the headlights off and hang out at a local lake or some other place for the rest of the night. Then we'd come back the next morning.

We had to attend church every Sunday. It was required and on Sunday morning there would be room checks. They would go through every room to make sure you were out of it and that your room was neat and tidy. I didn't like the fact that I had to be out of my room every Sunday morning. So I got around that. I'd get up at the same time as the other guys but as they headed out the door off to church, I'd hang back. Then I'd head back to my room and crawl back under the covers. When I heard the room police coming, I'd go into the closet, pull all my dirty clothes on top of me and hide on the closet floor.

The closet door was a bamboo screen kind of thing and you could see through the slats into the room. I remember my heart beating in my chest when the door opened and I would see this shadow of a person fall across the room. The light would go on and I'd watch them as they took a few steps into the room and look around. I was sure they could hear my heart pounding. Then they'd turn around, shut off the light, close the door and were on to the next room. I'd wait a little while, crouched under my dirty, smelly clothes and then slip out of the closet and enjoy a few more hours of sleep.

We had daily chapel. Attendance was required. In fact, outside the chapel doors were clip boards on which you signed your name as you walked in. I didn't like the fact that I had to go to chapel every day. So my buddies and I basically took turns playing hooky and having someone else sign us in.

We were forbidden to go to movies or concerts. We'd slip out once in a while and head to a town thirty miles away and see a new release. It's laughable when I think about it, but the band Chicago (a really hot group at the time) was giving a performance in Chicago, about a three hour drive from the school. A group of us petitioned the administration to be allowed to go to the concert. At first they denied our request, but as we protested louder, they gave in to us, with a stipulation. Upon our return from the performance we each had to write a paper explaining what impact the concert had on our spiritual life. Naturally each and every one of us wrote a very glowing report about how the music and the atmosphere actually enhanced our spiritual life. The administration wasn't too happy.

My friends were an interesting bunch. The school attracted many kids whose parents were in Christian work—pastors, teachers, missionaries—*lots* of MK's (missionary kids). They were more rebellious than I was! In fact, I became the unofficial "priest" of Alpha dorm the

year I was there. There were numerous Friday and Saturday nights when one of my friends would come in
drunk or on drugs or having slept with a girl from town
(affectionately known as a "townie") and they'd want to
pour out their heart to me about it. So with the bathroom
as our confession booth and with them frequently throwing up in the sink, I'd listen as they would tell me how
guilty they felt, promising never to do it again.

I could give more examples of rules that bothered me,
but let's move on. How these rules were affecting me and
my friends disturbed me. Intuitively I was sensing,
"Something's wrong with this picture. This isn't right." It
was distressing to me from a spiritual point of view because I found myself thinking, "If this is what Christianity
is all about, I'm not sure I've signed up for the right thing."
I had started off on my spiritual journey so full of joy and
life and vitality but over the months at school I was beginning to feel rebellious and stifled. Boxed-in, sat on, and
squashed would be good ways of describing how I was
feeling.

Legalism, or trying to live the life of faith by following
a bunch of man-made rules, was having a horrible effect
on my spiritual health. The idea that you are spiritual
and godly if you obey all the rules is the basic premise
behind legalism. Somehow I knew that was not right. I
couldn't figure it out that first year in college (thankfully
I spent only one year at the school) but I now know what's
wrong with that picture.

Rob Bell is the founding pastor of Mars Hill church in
Grand Rapids, Michigan. In his book *Velvet Elvis* he writes
about "shalom," the Hebrew word which means "peace."
Fundamentally, salvation—the act of God bringing us back
to Himself—is about bringing peace into unsettled lives.
Salvation is the process that enables people to begin living lives of wholeness and completeness, something that
sin has robbed us of the ability to do. Let me quote a section from Rob's book [Italics mine]:

"The point of the cross isn't forgiveness. Forgiveness leads to something much bigger: restoration. God isn't just interested in the covering over of our sins; God wants to make us into the people we were originally created to be. It's not just the removal of what's being held against us; it is God pulling us into the people he originally had in mind when he made us. This restoration is why Jesus always orients His message around becoming the kind of people who are generous and loving and compassionate. The goal here isn't simply to *not* sin. Our purpose is to increase the shalom in this world, *which is why approaches to the Christian faith that deal solely with not sinning always fail. They aim at the wrong thing. It is not about what you don't do.* The point is becoming more and more the kind of people God had in mind when we were first created."[35]

The entire thrust of legalism is to try to make Christians *not* do certain things, things which some group of people, somewhere, at some point in time determined were harmful to spiritual health. If we keep their rules then we are a spiritual person. Or let me say it another way: spirituality is condensed to nothing more than staying inside the box that some man has made.

But staying inside the box is not the key to healthy spirituality. A healthy life of faith is not found in *just avoiding* certain behaviors. When we try to live our life on that basis, I maintain that it sucks the very life of God out of us. The life of God, with us being the branches and Jesus being the vine from whom we get our very life energy, becomes nothing more than a dried up stream in the heat of the noonday desert sun.

We wither inside.

Our soul becomes barren, lifeless.

Our life becomes mechanical, perfunctory.

Jesus talked about a group of people who lived their lives like this. They were called the Pharisees. "These people draw near me with their mouths and honor me with their lips, but their hearts hold off and are far away from me. Uselessly do they worship me, for they teach as doctrines the commands of men."[36]

If you want an even darker picture of how destructive living your life like this can be read Matthew 23:1-33.[37] It's gruesome.

A healthy spiritual life is not found in making it our goal to not sin, but in making it our goal to run to Jesus—the author and source of our life and vitality and health and joy and peace and enthusiasm. Healthy spirituality is not about what we *don't do*—it's all about who we *run to*. These are two entirely different goals. And the end goal will always determine the path you take to reach them.

One brings life, the other death.

One binds us, the other sets us free.

Legalism is one of the great dream killers of the Christian life. Sadly, over the last seventy years or so, a good portion of the evangelical church in America has been fed a steady diet of this dream-killing teaching and the consequences have been tragic. I find so many churches that are lifeless and dying. I find so many Christians who are simply going through the motions of their faith, looking good on the outside but withered up on the inside. They seem to have no sense of destiny, no dreams that ignite their passions, no understanding of what God wants to do in them and through them to be a profound blessing to others. Something is not right with this picture.

As I said earlier, I only spent one year at that college. I had to get out. The rules, the regulations, the requirements, the stipulations were smothering me. I had to get out because I had a dream and I didn't want my dream to die.

---

[35] *Velvet Elvis*, Rob Bell, Zondervan Publications, Copyright © 2005, p. 108
[36] Matthew 15:7-9 *The Amplified Bible*

[37] Matthew 23:1-33

1 Then Jesus said to the crowds and to his disciples:

2 "The teachers of the law and the Pharisees sit in Moses' seat.

3 So you must obey them and do everything they tell you. But do not do what they do, for they do not practice what they preach.

4 They tie up heavy loads and put them on men's shoulders, but they themselves are not willing to lift a finger to move them.

5 "Everything they do is done for men to see: They make their phylacteries wide and the tassels on their garments long;

6 they love the place of honor at banquets and the most important seats in the synagogues;

7 they love to be greeted in the marketplaces and to have men call them 'Rabbi.'

8 "But you are not to be called 'Rabbi,' for you have only one Master and you are all brothers.

9 And do not call anyone on earth 'father,' for you have one Father, and he is in heaven.

10 Nor are you to be called 'teacher,' for you have one Teacher, the Christ.

11 The greatest among you will be your servant.

12 For whoever exalts himself will be humbled, and whoever humbles himself will be exalted.

13 "Woe to you, teachers of the law and Pharisees, you hypocrites! You shut the kingdom of heaven in men's faces.

14 You yourselves do not enter, nor will you let those enter who are trying to.

15 "Woe to you, teachers of the law and Pharisees, you hypocrites! You travel over land and sea to win a single convert, and when he becomes one, you make him twice as much a son of hell as you are.

16 "Woe to you, blind guides! You say, 'If anyone swears by the temple, it means nothing; but if anyone swears by the gold of the temple, he is bound by his oath.'

17 You blind fools! Which is greater: the gold, or the temple that makes the gold sacred?

18 You also say, 'If anyone swears by the altar, it means nothing; but if anyone swears by the gift on it, he is bound by his oath.'

19 You blind men! Which is greater: the gift, or the altar that makes the gift sacred?

20 Therefore, he who swears by the altar swears by it and by everything on it.

21 And he who swears by the temple swears by it and by the one who dwells in it.

22 And he who swears by heaven swears by God's throne and by the one who sits on it.

23 "Woe to you, teachers of the law and Pharisees, you hypocrites! You give a tenth of your spices—mint, dill and cummin. But you have neglected the more important matters of the law—justice, mercy and faithfulness. You should have practiced the latter, without neglecting the former.

24 You blind guides! You strain out a gnat but swallow a camel.

25 "Woe to you, teachers of the law and Pharisees, you hypocrites! You clean the outside of the cup and dish, but inside they are full of greed and self-indulgence.

26 Blind Pharisee! First clean the inside of the cup and dish, and then the outside also will be clean.

27 "Woe to you, teachers of the law and Pharisees, you hypocrites! You are like whitewashed tombs, which look beautiful on the outside but on the inside are full of dead men's bones and everything unclean.

28 In the same way, on the outside you appear to people as righteous but on the inside you are full of hypocrisy and wickedness.

29 "Woe to you, teachers of the law and Pharisees, you hypocrites! You build tombs for the prophets and decorate the graves of the righteous.

30 And you say, 'If we had lived in the days of our forefathers, we would not have taken part with them in shedding the blood of the prophets.'

31 So you testify against yourselves that you are the descendants of those who murdered the prophets.

32 Fill up, then, the measure of the sin of your forefathers!

33 "You snakes! You brood of vipers! How will you escape being condemned to hell?

 EIGHT

THE CALL

DO YOU BELIEVE in destiny? Do you believe that you personally have a destiny that you are supposed to fulfill while you live on this earth? I know a lot of people don't, but I do. As a Christian I always have. "'I know the plans I have for you,' says the Lord. 'Plans to prosper you and not to harm you, plans to give you hope and a future.'"[38] That verse has been a bedrock of belief for me since I first started on my spiritual journey. I think God's love for us is so strong, His investment in our lives so profound that there is simply no way to *not* believe that He has desires and plans for our lives that will ultimately bring us tremendous fulfillment and satisfaction.

A person's destiny can be summed up very nicely by the beginning words of Rick Warren's wildly popular book, *The Purpose Driven Life*. He begins by simply saying, "It's not about you."[39] Our purpose on this earth is not to live for ourselves, but to give ourselves away by investing in others, being concerned about others, serving others, and in the process being able to live our lives in such a way that God can work through us to be a blessing to others. When we do that, our lives bring glory to God. It's not about you. That truth is both simple and profound; yet how hard it is to live our lives like that.

Drilling down to a more specific and narrow focus I'd be curious how you would answer questions such as…

- Do you believe God has a particular person for you to marry?

- Do you believe God has a specific job you are to do?

- Do you believe God has a specific house or city you are to live in?

- Do you believe God has certain people that you are to engage with during any given day?

I answer questions like that this way: sometimes *yes*, sometimes *no*. How's that for a "don't-tie-me-down" response? Actually I am very serious. Just as there are billions of people in this world, each being made uniquely by God, with different gifts, talents, aptitudes, opportunities, stations in life, locations on this planet, and a wide variety of other factors, I believe God also has an infinite variety of plans for people's lives.

For some, He does have a specific person they are to marry. For others, there might be any number of individuals with whom a person could fall in love, marry, and spend the rest of their life very happily. For some God does have a specific job or career they are to work in. For others, based on the talents and abilities they've been given, God gives them the latitude of working in any number of fields, working a variety of different jobs and being able to find fulfillment in that variety. For some, because of purposes or reasons that are bigger than ourselves, God does have a specific home or city we are to live in for a period of time, or He brings someone across our path one day that we are specifically supposed to engage with.

All of this is part of the challenge and excitement of walking with God, day by day and moment by moment. Because just as I believe so strongly that God has a destiny for our lives, I also believe that He takes seriously His promise to guide us and lead us into that destiny.

I've never heard the audible voice of God. But just because He's never spoken to me out of the clouds with a James Earl Jones voice (that's how I imagine the voice of God) that doesn't mean He hasn't clearly made His plan known to me. I believe God is constantly speaking to us in big and small ways throughout our days. The problem with so many of us is that we are often so spiritually desensitized that we miss all His little clues and signals and nudges, with the result being we end up thinking God isn't at all interested in our lives. The reality is He's frustrated because we're not picking up on all the signals He's sending out.

For us to think that God isn't speaking just because we don't hear an audible voice is to totally underestimate and misunderstand how He communicates. There's a lot more to sound than just what meets the ear. Think of it like this: in terms of frequency, the human ear can hear sounds between 20 and 20,000 hertz or vibrations per second. If sounds are below 20 hertz—they are called *infrasonic*. Sounds above 20,000 hertz are *ultrasonic*. When we talk about sound most of us think about that small range that the human ear can hear. But it's outside that range where sound gets really interesting.

For example, infrasounds are fascinating. Infrasound has the power to cause headaches and earthquakes. According to zoologists, infrasound helps elephants predict changes in weather and helps birds navigate as they migrate. Infrasound can be used to locate underground oil and predict volcanic eruptions.

On the other end of the sound spectrum, ultrasound has the power to kill insects, track submarines, perform non-invasive surgery, topple buildings, clean jewelry, catalyze chemical reactions, heal damaged tissues, pasteurize milk, break up kidney stones, drill through hard materials, photograph unborn babies, and of course it's ultrasounds that drive dogs crazy.

So, there is a lot more to sound than just what meets the ear. There is also a lot more to God speaking to us than just hearing an audible voice. I've always been intrigued by a verse in the book of Job that says, "God does speak—now one way, now another—though man may not perceive it."[40] That verse captivates me. God *does* speak...even though we may not perceive it. So, if God doesn't talk to us audibly in His James Earl Jones voice, how does He speak with us today? He communicates with us in many more ways than we realize.

He speaks to us through,

   circumstances,

      signs,

         dreams,

            open and closed doors,

               the desires He puts in our hearts,

                  people,

                     and whispers or those internal
"nudgings" or "impressions" we sometimes get.

Let's focus on that last one—the whispers of God.
There's a great story in the Old Testament in I Kings 19.
In that chapter God appears to the prophet Elijah. At this
time, Elijah was running for his life because Jezebel was
chasing him. He was tired and hungry, depressed, and
feeling really sorry for himself. He says, "I've been zeal-
ous for the Lord God. The Israelites have rejected your
covenants, they've broken down your altars, they've put
your prophets to death. And I'm the only one left."[41] Then
God says "'Go out and stand on the mountain in the presence of the Lord, for the Lord is about to pass by.' Then a
great and powerful wind tore the mountains apart and
shattered the rocks before the Lord, but the Lord was not
in the wind. After the wind there was an earthquake, but
the Lord was not in the earthquake. After the earthquake
came a fire, but the Lord was not in the fire. And after
the fire came a gentle whisper."[42] It was in the whisper
that God spoke to Elijah.

I love Margaret Feinberg's explanation of why God
whispers. Lighting and thunder are more impressive but
Feinberg says, "To hear someone's whisper you need to
be near him or her. Whispering doesn't work very well if
the person you are speaking to is on the other side of the
room. God isn't content with a long-distance relationship."
She continues, "The internal voice is like an audible voice,
except you do not hear it with your ears. Instead, you

hear it with your spirit. The internal audible voice is a thought, phrase, or concept that rings clear within your being."[43]

Early on in my Christian journey there were two times when I believe God sent out some signals to me concerning the direction my life should take. They both took the form of whisperings. They were "thoughts" or "concepts" that started to ring clear within me. The first was when I began to sense that I should go into the ministry (remember I had planned on becoming an orthopedic surgeon). The second was when I sensed that I should start a church.

Having not really been raised in a strong church environment, I was exposed to a whole new world when I decided to follow Christ at the age of seventeen. I got heavily involved in a local church, and that was a whole new experience for me. The thought of being a pastor or being involved in some kind of full time Christian work had never even crossed my mind.

But very shortly after I became a Christian and had gotten involved in a church, I began having these "nudgings" or "inner impressions" that I was supposed to go into the ministry. Finally after months of having these thoughts, and after praying about it a lot and talking with some people, I determined that I needed to pursue this career direction, even though I knew nothing about it. It was at that point, as I mentioned at the beginning of the previous chapter, that I went to one of the ministers of the church I was attending and asked him what I needed to do to go into the ministry. So, I picked my college and was off and running. During my college years those feelings continued to grow stronger, and as the years passed I became very convinced that I had found my life's calling.

Then there was the second time those nudgings began. As I was finishing up college and planning on attending seminary I began to sense that God was telling me that upon graduating from seminary, I needed to start a church. Again, that was the furthest thing from my mind. The typical path that most newly graduated seminary students take is to send out resumes to churches that are looking for an associate pastor, or smaller churches that are looking for a senior, preaching pastor.

But all through my time in seminary I just kept having these *feelings* that I was not supposed to take that path, but rather I was to start a new church, from scratch. It was like God was whispering that thought over and over again into my spirit. This was a daunting thought initially, and in talking with a few of my professors from seminary, I didn't get much encouragement. In fact, in essence they all said it was a pretty foolish thing to consider doing. But in spite of their reservations, I just couldn't shake the thought that this was what I needed to do.

I remember telling people at the time that this was something I *had* to do. Sure, I could find an existing church and take an associate pastor position or become the senior pastor of a small church, but if I took that path, I knew I would spend the rest of my life wondering *what would have happened if?* If I didn't at least *try* and begin a new church as I felt God was directing me to do, would I spend the rest of my life living with regret and wondering about what might have been? I also rationalized that if it didn't work out, I could always fall back to plan "B" and go find some church to work in. I'm not being overly dramatic when I say that in essence, the next thirty years of my life were shaped once those two issues were resolved. My destiny was set.

Those were exciting days. My mind was kept busy planning, writing, thinking, strategizing about the new church. So many things had to be done. Finding a location, designing and printing promotional material, getting the 501 (C) 3 status from the IRS, and figuring out how it was all going to be paid for. In the only way I knew, I tried to let people know that a new church was beginning by going door to door. I got a map of the city and systematically began to canvass neighborhoods in the area of the new church. Faithfully, for the first two years on Monday, Wednesday, and Friday afternoons I would grab a stack of brochures and walk the neighborhoods, ringing doorbells, talking with people who would answer, and leaving a brochure where nobody was home.

On one occasion I was literally chased down the street by a Jewish woman in her bathrobe who was terribly upset that I had left a piece of Christian literature at her door. The process was long, tedious, and overall very ineffective. I wore out five pair of shoes during those first two years, but it was the only way I knew how to get the word out. So I just kept at it. The ignorance and enthusiasm of youth, bulldog tenacity, and a definite call from God were what kept me going.

But even with all the excitement and zeal I had for this dream, my struggle was never very far from the center of my mind. I kept having a recurring thought. Initially it was something that I didn't pay much attention to, but over the years it has been something I've become more and more focused on, and for which unfortunately, I have never been able to get a clear answer. The thought was this: How do I reconcile my calling into ministry and my calling to start a church with the fact that I have a major struggle which, from an evangelical perspective, should immediately disqualify me for ministry? This has been a *huge* issue for me over the years. There have been so many times I've wondered, "Did I misunderstand the voice of God? Did I just *think* He was directing me to go into ministry? Was it just my mind playing tricks on me that I thought He was leading me to begin a new church? Should I have stayed the course and become a physician?" At least that's a profession where a person's sexuality doesn't prevent him from being a very competent, good surgeon, or put him in danger of losing his job.

It became an even greater internal struggle as the church began to grow and become quite prosperous.

God's hand of blessing seemed to be resting on the work in which we were engaged. I don't want to bore you with statistics, but Grace Chapel had turned into a large church with sizeable assets by the time I resigned. For the very first service we had in 1979, thirty-five people showed up. That included me, my wife, our daughter, my parents, Char's brother and his wife, my uncle and his wife and their three children. Attendance went downhill after that. It actually took us some months to hit that 35 number again.

By the time 2006 rolled around, we had around 1,200 active families that were part of the church. That's how we measured the size of Grace—by the number of family units. If you figure that an average family unit has three persons in it, the church had around 3,600 folks that would be considered regular attendees. Our annual budget continued to grow each year from around $80,000 back in 1979 to the 4 to 5 million dollar range. We owned some prime land and property valued at over $20 million. We had a counseling center, we had planted another church in a neighboring community that was doing well, there were dozens upon dozens of programs and ministries designed for people of all ages—men, women, children. There was a paid staff of over fifty people working in a variety of departments and various areas. It was a thriving enterprise.

For a new church that had started in the music room of a junior high school, with Char and me hauling in a couple of fake plants and some hymn books, to grow as it did—that was a God thing. I don't have any other way to describe it, because honestly I felt that it certainly wasn't because of me. How could it be with my struggle that constantly had me feeling, "I have no business being in ministry in the first place"? It reminds me of what President Warren Harding once said. Historians agree that Harding was one of the worst presidents in American history. After he got into office he is quoted as having said, "I am not fit for this office and never should have been here." That's how I've felt. When everything was said and done, the success that Grace Chapel enjoyed was totally and completely a God thing. It was blessed simply because He chose to bless it.

This is an overpowering thought for me. For thirty years, I've had the deep seated belief that I wasn't worthy of the success that I was achieving. I wasn't worthy of the honor and respect that I was being given. I wasn't worthy of the title "pastor." Never. My sexual struggle continually kept me from embracing and enjoying what God was doing in me, through me and around me. Everything in my life was processed through the lens of my sexuality and I just kept having the thought, "If people only knew, I'd be kicked out of this club faster than you could say 'good-riddance.'"

All of us are broken people but God uses broken people. For purposes that are beyond me and for reasons I don't fully understand, He chose to use me, a very broken vessel, to accomplish His desire. That's God. We are broken jars of clay, yet God is the potter who can fashion us into useable vessels of service. One of the emails I received after my resignation highlighted this struggle between my call and my sexuality. The individual, a man in our church wrote, "I don't know why you struggle with homosexuality and why the Lord would put you in the ministry. It seems a cruel hoax to me. This I do know— you have been a beloved pastor and you are welcome to share my pew any time. I accept you as you are because Jesus accepts me 'just as I am.'" Then he went on to say, "The church does have a way of shooting its wounded…it's a shameful legacy."

One of the things I had fun with during seminary was trying to figure out a name for the church. I had all sorts of ideas. I wish I could remember some of them now. Ultimately there were two things that I knew I wanted the name of the church to reflect. Regardless of how big the church would ever become, I wanted the name to convey an idea of smallness, of coziness if you will, of intimacy. Thus I settled on the word CHAPEL. That word had a nice, warm, inviting ring to me.

The other thing I wanted the name to convey was some vital aspect of the Christian faith that would be central to our teaching and belief. I toyed with the names FAITH Chapel, HOPE Chapel, LOVE Chapel (that sounded a little too much like a place in Vegas), but ultimately settled on the word I thought most profoundly reflected God's attitude towards people—GRACE. God is so much a God of grace. I needed it and was experiencing it, and I wanted our church to be a place where people could experience it as well. I wanted the church to be a place where hurting, broken, disillusioned, disenfranchised people could come and instead of finding judgment, condemnation, and guilt, they could find the peace, forgiveness and acceptance of a gracious God who loves them deeply and longs to be in relationship with them. Thus, GRACE CHAPEL became the name of our church.

[38] Jeremiah 29:11

[39] *The Purpose Driven Life*, Rick Warren, Zondervan Publications, Copyright © 2002, p. 17

[40] Job 33:14

[41] I Kings 19:10

[42] I Kings 19:11-12

[43] *God Whispers: Learning to Hear His Voice*, Margaret Feinberg, Relevant Books, Copyright © 2002

 NINE

INTEGRITY, SIN AND GRACE

IN THE FALL OF 2006 the scandal surrounding Pastor Ted Haggard became national news. I don't know how much media coverage it received in other markets around the country. I know it was big time on the nightly national news and in magazines, but it became *really* big news in Colorado. Pastor Haggard was the founding pastor of New Life Church in Colorado Springs, a church with approximately 14,000 members. He was also the president of the thirty-million member National Association of Evangelicals.

Colorado had a ballot initiative in the upcoming November election which would ban gay marriage and Pastor Haggard had been a vocal supporter of the proposed amendment. A male prostitute by the name of Mike Jones contacted the media indicating that he had been having sexual relations with Haggard over a three year period and that he had also sold Haggard methamphetamine. Jones indicated that he became upset when he discovered that Haggard was preaching against gay marriage and then going behind the scenes and having gay sex.

This situation affected me deeply because of the way it played itself out in the media. At first Haggard denied involvement with Jones, then admitted it, denied his drug use, then admitted it. The whole sordid story was fodder for rabid news organizations that were anxious to dig up any dirt they could on this successful and well respected Christian leader. Sadly, the way Pastor Haggard handled the situation only fed their frenzy.

It also affected me because it hit so close to home. It hit close to home geographically because Colorado Springs is only a forty-five minute drive from my home in

Denver. It hit close to home because of my own struggle. As the story unfolded, the knots in my stomach grew bigger with each passing day, with every article I read, and news report I saw. Even though I'd never met Pastor Haggard, I felt an incredible amount of empathy for him and his shell-shocked wife and family. I kept putting myself and my wife and kids in their place and it was a horrifying thought.

I already had my sermon prepared for the following Sunday, but I was so deeply affected by what was happening that I couldn't proceed with what I had planned to do. So on Saturday, I went into the office, scrapped the sermon I had planned to give and began jotting down some rambling thoughts that reflected how I was processing all that I was hearing and observing.

Many years ago I developed the habit of manuscripting my sermons. In other words, I would write them verbatim—word for word, and then deliver it that way. That allowed me to be sure that before I went into the pulpit I would say what I wanted to say, how I wanted to say it. Because this particular message was so last minute, I didn't have the chance to do that like I normally would. However, I wrote my thoughts down and what you'll read here is fairly accurate as to how I delivered it.

When I first thought about writing a book one of the things that immediately came to my mind was this sermon. At the time I determined that if a book ever became a reality, I wanted to include a CD copy of this sermon for you. Ultimately, that wasn't very practical but I do have it posted on my website for you to listen to.[44]

I would like to encourage you to consider taking the time to *listen* to the message. It's about thirty minutes long. The words you'll read here are close but not a verbatim copy of the sermon I gave. You can read it and understand basically what I said, but part of the reason I wrote this book was because I wanted people to know my heart and I wanted you to know my spirit, and sometimes that can't adequately be conveyed just through some words on a page. There is a pathos or emotion that often comes through our spoken words that can't be captured by the written word. This message was a very emotional sermon for me. I had a difficult time keeping myself collected while I was giving it. I had a raging storm going on inside me. Perhaps by listening to it, you can understand me a little better.

With that being said, here is the sermon I delivered to the congregation of Grace Chapel on November 5, 2006, simply entitled, "Integrity, Sin and Grace."

INTRODUCTION

I want to suspend the series we've been in on the Holy Spirit for today and have opportunity to talk with you about some of the events of this past week and share some thoughts surrounding the unfolding story about Ted Haggard. I realize my thoughts may be rambling and disjointed and if they seem that way I apologize. I came into the office yesterday to put some finishing touches on the message that you have the outline for. And I just had this nudging thought that this isn't right. It isn't right to just continue on with business as usual when this kind of situation has confronted us. So I jotted down some thoughts.

I thought long and hard about this—do I say nothing and we just continue on as if nothing was happening? And I didn't feel that was the right thing to do. But obviously I haven't had a lot of time to prepare so my thoughts might seem a little jumbled, and if they do I'm sorry. I also realize that I may not say some things about this situation that you think I should say. And if that's the case please extend some grace and realize that these are my thoughts as of yesterday. Through this I was really praying that I would reflect the heart of Jesus.

Obviously at this time we don't know all that is true, but as of last night apparently the accusations were accurate and he was released from his duties at New Life, and while we don't know all the facts, we do know that it's a mess. And I think we have to guard about being judgmental and this is a point in time when as Christians we need to choose our words very carefully and our actions be very wise.

I don't know about you...I'm sure some of you read the story, brushed it off and went on with your life, but the last couple, three days have been extremely hard for me personally. I've had a lot of emotions, I've had a lot of knots in my stomach, and you probably have a lot of emotions about it as well. And if there is any emotion that you should have right now as a Christian, it should be one of sadness. And that sadness should drive you to prayer. And to be in prayer for everybody that is involved in that situation. It's just another reminder to us that we are in a spiritual battle and often times the people who are out on the front lines become more of a target for the enemy. So I can't begin to encourage you strongly enough to be in prayer for everyone involved in this situation.

Some of the thoughts that I have:

INTEGRITY

I think we all realize that integrity is very important—and I define integrity as being the same on the outside as you are on the inside. The idea of integrity is that of wholeness. And one of the end results of the Christian faith is that it should help move all of us towards a greater sense of wholeness in our lives, of being people of integrity—of being the same on the outside as we are on the inside.

But as you know, this is a lifelong struggle for those who desire to follow Jesus. We all come to the cross as broken people and we get up from the foot of the cross and as we begin to live our lives as Christians—a whole new journey begins. It really does. But I have to tell you that one of the mysteries of our faith, and it is something that I have never quite been able to figure out or understand, is why it is that God deals with different people in the different ways that He does.

For example, sometimes when a person comes to the Lord and they have a broken area in their life, it's almost like instantaneously and miraculously that broken area is healed. Maybe they struggle with alcoholism and God miraculously sets them free. Maybe they struggle with pornography and God instantaneously sets them free from that. Maybe they struggle with a bad temper and all of a sudden it's gone. Maybe they struggle with a bad mouth and it's gone. And there is almost this kind of instantaneous deliverance for some people and God heals them of their brokenness. And then sometimes, for a lot of people, it's a long painful process of being healed from their brokenness and it takes years and years and years. And sometimes it takes a lot of counseling and therapy, reading, fasting, praying and just a wide variety of other things, but eventually after years and years of pressing forward and pushing through, they find that their brokenness is healed. But it just takes a long, long time.

And then for some reason there are some people for whom an area of brokenness in their life is never healed. They live with it until the day they die. I view Paul's thorn in the flesh as being that way. Whatever that was Paul prayed three times, he sought God earnestly and said please take this away from me and finally God said, "Paul, enough. You can stop praying about that because I'm not going to change it. It's going to be there in your life and you are going to need to learn that My grace is sufficient for you and My power is going to be made perfect in your weakness." And so he lived with it, I guess, until the day he died. So it is a mystery to me. I don't understand why God deals with different people in the different ways as it relates to those areas of brokenness.

But, regardless of that, the fact is we are all broken people and part of that brokenness is that we struggle to be people of integrity—to be the same on the outside as we are on the inside.

And my feeling is that the vast majority of us, if we're honest with ourselves, most of us probably struggle in some areas of our life with integrity. Most of us, if the truth were known, wear masks to try and hide some of our brokenness. And we do so for a variety of reasons. We all want to be loved and accepted and I think many feel that if others knew them for who they really were, they would no longer be loved or accepted. So we put on our masks. And try to be someone that people can love and accept. Sometimes we wear masks because we want to appear more perfect than we are, but the reality is all of us are so very imperfect. We don't want people to know that maybe we struggle with sexual sin, or pornography, or being abusive to our families, or being a person of greed, or being an overzealous workaholic so that we become a disenfranchised, uninvolved part of our family. Whatever it may be, we don't want people to know that about us and so we put on a mask.

But as I think that through, this whole issue speaks to the fact that fundamentally something isn't right in the Christian community. When a Christian…and it doesn't matter whether it's a well-known pastor or just a regular church-going Christian, but when somebody in the family of God feels like they have no one to talk to—no one to confide in—no one in whom they can place their trust—it really prevents us from being people of integrity…of being people of wholeness. And so what happens is, we end up living behind our masks in our own isolated pain and loneliness.

And somehow, and I don't know what the answers are, and I don't know how it's going to happen, but somehow we have to get better at being men and women who are living our lives in an atmosphere of grace—where we can say to each other—it's OK. It's OK for you to tell me who you really are and I am not going to think any less of you regardless of what you tell me. Because the fact is, we're all in this together. And I know it sounds trite, and you've heard it a million times, but it still doesn't make the reality of it any less true—Christians never claim to be perfect—just forgiven. And James reminds us that we all stumble in many ways.

So that's my first thought.

SIN

Something else that this has reminded me of is how careful we have to be to not rank sin. As I have told you before, it distresses me so much that the Christian community is really the only army that shoots its wounded. We have a tendency to start shooting those who have fallen rather than try to nurse them and nurture them back to health and wholeness.

It says in Proverbs 6:16 "There are six things the LORD hates, yes, seven are an abomination to Him; a proud look, a lying tongue, hands that shed innocent blood, a heart that devises wicked plans, feet that are swift in running to evil, a false witness who speaks lies, and one who sows discord among brethren." So you take that list: pride, lying, murder, causing dissension, knowingly defaming a person by lying about their character…those are the kinds of things God hates. They are an abomination to Him. Those are really strong words, *hate* and *abomination*. Then in addition to a few things that God hates, I think there are a lot of things that make God very sad.

Paul says in I Corinthians 6:9-10 "Do you not know that the unrighteous will not inherit the kingdom of God? Do not be deceived; neither the immoral, nor idolaters, nor adulterers, nor sexual perverts, nor thieves, nor the greedy, nor drunkards, nor revilers, nor robbers will inherit the kingdom of God." I think we have to be really careful in picking out what sins we think are the worst and what sins aren't. Picking out what we might call lifestyle sins vs. once-in-a while sins. Once-in-a-while sins that affect even good Christians, we can blow off with the phrase, "We all fall sometime." Lifestyle sins however, at least the ones we're not committing, we have a tendency to condemn very loudly. It's interesting to me what Paul puts on that list, because right up there with the immoral and the adulterers and the sexual perverts are the idolaters, the thieves, the greedy, the drunkards, the robbers.

Why is it that we are so prone to pick and choose which sins we'll say are the worst and which ones aren't? I'm afraid that usually, the worst sins, in our minds anyway, are the ones that other people commit, and the lesser sins are the ones that we tend to commit. We get up in arms for example about someone who is immoral or a pedophile or somebody who commits some kind of sexual sin.

But why do we always seem to be silent about some of the other sins—the sin of idolatry for example—that so many Christians love someone or something far more than they love God and their lifestyle reflects that idolatry, but we say nothing? Why is it that we can be so forgiving about someone who says, "Hi, I'm Bob and I'm an alcoholic," and we say, "Hi Bob. We hope the 12 step program works for you. Poor man. You must have had a bad childhood to drive you to drink." Why is it that we say nothing about the robber or the thief, and yet God says in Malachi that every person who is not honoring God with their finances is robbing Him? But of course, we don't want to go there.

Even more close to home, why do we gloss over the issue of adultery the way we do? You know Jesus said "Everyone who divorces his wife for any reason except sexual immorality causes her to commit adultery; and whoever marries a woman who is divorced commits adultery." (Matthew 5:31-32) In the church, which reflects society, 50 percent of the people have been divorced and of those who have divorced, about 85 percent of those folks have remarried. And the fact is many of those divorces were not because of adultery, which is a legitimate cause to get a divorce, but simply because of what we call "irreconcilable" differences. And that has a wide range of things underneath it. And those people who have now remarried are committing adultery. But it's so prevalent in the church that we end up saying, "Well, I'm under God's grace, He's forgiven me, and you don't understand my personal situation and I'm so much happier now and the kids are so much better off."

You know I have honestly wondered over the last couple of years, what causes more damage to a society, the two to three percent of the people in a society that are gay or the 50 percent of people in society who have been married and divorced, re-married and the kids, the poor kids, are experiencing all the ramifications that all that garbage involves. And we're seeing it in the upcoming generations.

That's my second thought.

GRACE

The final thought I have is this: I hope we can all work hard to be people of grace. Grace and mercy are so fundamental to our faith. Grace is God not giving us what we deserve and mercy is God giving us what we don't deserve. Grace is God looking down at us and saying, "You know, because they've all broken my laws many times and in many ways, they deserve my punishment. But I'm going to be merciful, and instead of punishing them, I realize they are harassed and helpless, like sheep without a shepherd and I love them, and I'm going to punish Jesus, My only Son, instead."

It's kind of a catch phrase that we use today, "We have to hate the sin but love the sinner." But, as Einstein said and Christ demonstrated, "You cannot simultaneously say that you love someone and use your power against them."

Christ did not use His power to legislate against the sinful people of His day. Instead He partied with them. Jesus didn't condemn the woman caught with her skirt up—literally. Instead He embarrassed her detractors by saying that anyone who had not sinned could throw the first stone at her. And not a single stone was ever thrown. Christ didn't raise money for His cause by claiming that those involved in the sinful lifestyles of His day were ganging up to destroy the family. Instead He invited them to be His friends and His followers.

So let's work hard—and it takes hard work because it goes against our natural grain many times—but let's work hard at extending the same grace to others that we've been given. You know, I'm really thankful that I don't have to be perfect. That's a hard standard to try and live up to. If we were perfect, we wouldn't need a Savior and we wouldn't need salvation would we? But I am so thankful that my Jesus was perfect and I have His righteousness. I have His righteousness.

This passage in Matthew 18 is the parable of the unforgiving servant. I want to read it to you. It's kind of a haunting parable to me.

> "Then Peter came to Jesus and asked, "Lord, how many times shall I forgive my brother when he sins against me? Up to seven times?" Jesus answered, "I tell you, not seven times, but seventy-seven times. Therefore, the kingdom of heaven is like a king who wanted to settle accounts with his servants. As he began the settlement, a man who owed him ten thousand talents [multiplied millions of dollars in today's economy] was brought to him. Since he was not able to pay, the master ordered that he and his wife and his children and all that he had be sold to repay the debt. The servant fell on his knees before him. 'Be patient with me,' he begged, 'and I will pay back everything.' The servant's

master took pity on him, canceled the debt and let him go. But when that servant went out, he found one of his fellow servants who owed him a hundred denarii [about ten bucks]. He grabbed him and began to choke him. 'Pay back what you owe me!' he demanded. His fellow servant fell to his knees and begged him, 'Be patient with me, and I will pay you back.' But he refused. Instead, he went off and had the man thrown into prison until he could pay the debt. When the other servants saw what had happened, they were greatly distressed and went and told their master everything that had happened. Then the master called the servant in. 'You wicked servant,' he said, 'I canceled all that debt of yours because you begged me to. Shouldn't you have had mercy on your fellow servant just as I had on you?' In anger his master turned him over to the jailers to be tortured, until he should pay back all he owed. This is how my heavenly Father will treat each of you unless you forgive your brother from your heart." (Matthew 18:21-35)

Folks, I don't want to be judged by God for being like that wicked servant, someone who has been forgiven of my own sin and my own sinful lifestyle but someone who becomes unwilling to forgive the lifestyles of my fellow human beings.

CONCLUSION

I leave you with this thought. We often put the work of Christ on the cross in very theological terms. He was our substitute, He was the propitiation for our sins, and He was the atoning sacrifice for my sins. Substitute, propitiation, atonement—those are big words. Those words can often hide the pathos behind the cross. So why don't we put it in real practical terms? When Jesus died on that cross, He bore the sin of the world in His body. And for that brief moment on the cross when God turned His face away from His only beloved Son and Jesus cried out, "My God, my God, why have you forsaken me?" For that brief moment in time, Jesus became what you are. "He who knew no sin became sin for us so that in him we might become the righteousness of God." (II Corinthians 5:21)

Jesus became what you are. If you're a thief, Jesus became a thief. If you are a murderer, Jesus became a murderer. If you are an adulterer, Jesus became an adulterer. If you are a gossip seeking to tear down people's lives, Jesus became a gossip, tearing down people's lives. If you're an alcoholic, Jesus became an alcoholic. If you're a drug user, Jesus became a drug user. If you're a self-serving, materialistic person filled with greed, Jesus became a greedy, self-serving, materialistic person. If you are gay, Jesus became gay. If you're a self-righteous little Pharisee who says, "I'm glad I've never done any of those things in my life" then Jesus became a self-righteous Pharisee saying, "I'm glad I've never done any of those things in my life." As He hung on that cross He became everyone's sin.

And why did He do that? Why did He become all those things and more? "Because God so loved the world that he gave his only begotten Son, that whoever (it doesn't matter who you are) whoever believes in him shall not perish but have eternal life. For God didn't send his son into the world to condemn the world, but to save the world through him." (John 3:16-17) Amen.

---

[44] To listen to the message, "Integrity, Sin and Grace" go to the following link: http://www.PhoenixRisingCoach.com/IntegritySinandGrace.php

 TEN

RESIGNATION

WHEN JAPAN ATTACKED the United States by bombing Pearl Harbor, President Franklin D. Roosevelt delivered an address to the nation the next day by saying, "Yesterday December 7, 1941—a date which will live in infamy—the United States of America was suddenly and deliberately attacked by naval and air forces of the Empire of Japan."

Interestingly, my official resignation happened on December 7, 2006. But my actual day of infamy was two days earlier, Tuesday, December 5. The day started out just like most others. I arrived at the church around 7:30 and as I walked into my office I noticed that one of our associate pastors was already in talking with our executive pastor. I had barely set my briefcase down and started getting organized for the day when a knock came on my door and the two men were standing there asking if they could come in.

Once we got seated, it was with great difficulty that our associate pastor looked at me and said, "This is very hard for me. I received an anonymous call last night expressing concern for you and our church. The caller indicated that there was someone he knew who was planning to go to the news media with information about you that would be similar to what happened with Ted Haggard." One of the things we had at the church was what we called Pastor on Call (POC). Each night a different pastor would take a cell phone that people could call for emergencies. And that is why this particular pastor received the phone call that he did. He went on to explain that it was a very short call, and that the caller was very concerned. There was no animosity or hatred expressed by him, in fact, the caller ended his conversation by praying for me and our church.

And that was that.

Of course, over the years I'd thought many, many times about what I would do if my secret became public knowledge. As you might expect, I had a variety of thoughts as to different ways of dealing with the revelation. But something solidified for me when I saw the debacle and spectacle of Ted Haggard's revelation, his subsequent resignation and how it was played out in the news media. Remember, that happened only about five weeks prior. I remember thinking at the time. "If that ever happens to me, I'm going to just come clean, tell my story, resign, and be done with it." The last thing in the world I wanted was for my family and our church to have to experience what I witnessed with him.

Unfortunately, it didn't work out that way.

I excused the associate pastor and began a very difficult, heart to heart conversation with our executive pastor. I started at the beginning when I was five and walked him through my life, the continual struggle that I had, my becoming a Christian and the many things I did as a believer to try to get my issue "fixed," the hundreds of nights I cried myself to sleep begging God to change me, the three different times I'd gone to counselors in an attempt to have them offer some insights or help, the massive amounts of reading that I had done on the subject, the guilt, shame, and remorse that I lived with. I also acknowledged that over the years that I had fallen, and given in to my desires.

He listened attentively but it's what he said that I'll always remember. Almost the very first words out of his mouth were, "You need to pray about resigning." That was his way of saying, "You need to resign." A part of me knew he was right, yet there was also something deeper within me that felt that there should be a better way.

That conversation started what would be a whirlwind of meetings and quickly unfolding events which only six days later would culminate in announcing my resignation to our church family. I immediately tried to get in touch with three men whom I felt I needed to have come alongside me for guidance. Two were out of town and unavailable. One was gracious enough to meet me that very afternoon.

I drove across town with our executive pastor to this gentleman's office, and as I had done earlier laid out the entire story. After listening to my story the first words out of his mouth were, "I can't imagine what it's been like for you to have to carry this burden all by yourself for so many years." With that he got up from his chair, came over and wrapped me in his arms. And I began to cry.

Telling Char was obviously the most difficult thing I've ever had to do. Over the years I had thought a lot about how she might respond to this revelation. Char is an incredibly spiritual, strong woman yet I really had no idea how she would react to this. During the course of our marriage she had made some comments about homosexuality which led me to think that I could very well be headed for divorce if and when she ever discovered my secret. So I began to brace for the worst.

The problem was the timing. Char was the director of our Women's Ministry program at Grace and every year in December she held a huge Christmas outreach event. It ran for two nights and around 600 to 700 women attended. It was a very attention consuming event for Char and she needed all her wits to stay focused and centered on what was going on those two nights. The first night it was held was on Monday, December 4. The second night was Tuesday, December 5. It was that morning of the fifth that all this began to unfold. I couldn't talk to Char that day about it—I didn't want her to have this bomb dropped into her lap and then have her go and host the event that evening, all the while pretending to be in a joyous Christmas spirit.

So I waited. She had already left for the event by the time I arrived home from work. I went to bed about 10:00 and she got home around midnight. I wasn't asleep when she came in but pretended that I was. She crawled into bed and I waited until I heard her heavy breathing and then I slipped out and went downstairs. I spent the rest of the night in the family room, awake, my head spinning out of control, my heart pounding because of the conversation I knew I was going to have in the morning. I waited and waited and waited. Time goes so slowly in the darkness of night. I didn't think daylight was ever going to come. Finally around 6:30 a.m. she came downstairs. I said, "Honey, we need to talk." By the way, those five words have always struck terror in my heart when Char has said them to me. I think they do for most men actually. They're awful words to have to hear.

She came over and sat down next to me on the couch and I took her hand and began. We stayed on the couch for about 3 ½ hours that morning. And even now, as I think about it, it brings tears to my eyes, but the thing that struck me the most about Char's response was that during that entire time on the couch, she never let go of my hand. And her words surprised me. Though in shock and now with her head spinning as well, she affirmed her love for me, her sadness that I had lived with this secret for so long, her faith in God, and her confidence that we would get through this—together. I don't mean to sound frivolous at this very serious juncture but I mean it with all my heart when I say that I married way above my head. I really did.

At this point let me address a question some may have. Some might be thinking, "How could she stay with him? Why would she continue to stay married after what he's done and his deceit?" My marriage and our relationship are very personal and there are some things that I choose not to get in to. Every marriage has storms that have to be weathered. We are getting through ours. The bottom line is—we love each other. We also *like* each other. We enjoy being with one another. When we have free time, we like to spend it together. We seldom raise our voices in anger. We've never really had any type of major fight. I've never spent a night on the couch. We laugh—a lot. We've tried to support each other in our dreams, aspirations, hopes, and goals. We encourage one another. We listen to each other. We've invested over thirty years going through life together. We were partners in the church endeavor. We were partners in raising our children. We are each other's best friend. Our marriage has a lot going for it.

But in addition we have God as part of our lives. He can give supernatural strength to get through situations which, from a human perspective, would be disastrous. Char's faith, spiritual maturity, strength, and commitment make her an absolutely amazing woman. There is no doubt about that. I realize she has responded to this situation in a way that many women would not. But it is because of her response that I have been the recipient of a flesh and blood example of forgiveness and grace being extended to me and it makes me love her even more.

Let's come back to the story. Over the next two days, I confided in a few other key individuals whom I felt needed to know at this early stage and then at a hastily called Board meeting on Thursday night, Char and I sat with a group of about fifteen men and I shared my story and announced my immediate resignation. On Friday morning I did the same thing. Only this time it was with our staff. Our precious staff. There were probably thirty of the fifty or so staff members there. We gathered in our chapel and I told them I was leaving and why. There were a lot of tears and a lot of hugs and a lot of prayers and after they were finished praying for Char and me, we walked out of the chapel, got into our car and left the church campus. At that point everything seemed surreal.

One of the biggest issues I had to face was how to tell our church family. Early on in the week as things were being processed it was thought that I would simply write a letter not detailing the reason for the resignation but simply announcing that effective immediately I would be resigning due to personal reasons. I drafted a letter. It was reviewed and revised by a handful of individuals and a somewhat final draft was settled on. But as the week wore on both Char and I felt more and more unsettled with this plan of action. After 28 years, was that the best way to leave our church family? And besides, we reasoned, how would you ever keep the reason for the resignation a secret? It wouldn't happen.

I finally concluded that it wasn't fair to take that approach. Just as I had laid out the grim story to others throughout the week, I realized I needed to be honest and do the same thing with the entire church. It was the only right thing to do. The problem was, I couldn't personally do that four times on Sunday (three morning services and a fourth one in the evening). I just couldn't. That would take an emotional toll that I didn't think I could bear. So we did a video. I told my story with Char sitting by my side and Char and I both shared our love and heart for the people of Grace Chapel and the future of the church. It was the video that was shown at the four Sunday services.

Three other very difficult conversations were still before me and had to take place before Sunday. Our two daughters and their husbands. And my parents.

Char took the lead with our girls. I will be forever grateful to her for the way she stepped into this crisis situation and talked with our precious daughters. She made the phone calls and laid out the story. Understandably, the initial response was shock and disbelief, but true-to-form, both of our girls, who are very mature, godly women, responded with grace and love.

A week later we had both couples over to the house and showed them the video. We used that as a springboard to launch into our discussion with them. I want you to know something about my sons-in-law. They are two great, godly men and we are so blessed to have them as part of our family. We couldn't have asked for two better men to marry our girls. They are both such a joy and delight to us. One of them was raised on a farm in Kansas. He's a solid, salt-of-the-earth kind of guy, hardworking and very used to sucking it up and doing what needs to be done to get the job finished. I wasn't sure how Josh would respond to all this, but his reaction shocked me. After we finished showing them the video, Josh began to cry (kind of unusual for a tough farm boy) and through sobs he was barely able to get out the words, "I'm so sorry that you had to go through all this alone." We've got great kids.

Then there were my parents. As it concerned them, we decided to go see them and tell them in person (they live about two hours away). On Friday I called and my mom answered and I said,

"Hi, Mom."

"Well, hi, Paul. How are you?"

"Not so good."

"What's wrong?"

"I wanted you to know I've resigned my position at the church."

"Oh, no!"

"I was wondering if Char and I could come up on Sunday morning and see you. We'll probably be spending a few days with you if that's O.K."

That's pretty much all that I said on the phone. But early Sunday morning we took off, driving by the church as the first service was being held, praying for what was going on inside. And praying for what we were going to have to do in a few hours.

We arrived at their house, said our hellos, hit the kitchen to scrounge through the refrigerator (a habit we got into a long time ago) and settled into their living room. With my heart feeling like it was stuck in my throat I launched into yet another telling of my story, which by this time I was very, very tired of telling. The emotional toll it was taking on me each time was indescribable. They both listened carefully but obviously it was hitting them pretty hard.

Again, it was with my parents (my father in particular) that I was totally unsure of what kind of reaction I would receive. Because of my dad's feelings about homosexuality, I was fully prepared that I might be disowned from the family. But again, their reaction was surprising. After I'd finished, some of the first words out of my dear mom's mouth were, "I shouldn't have spent so much time in the kitchen." Bless her heart, she was already blaming herself. My dad began to cry and he got up from his chair, came over, embraced me with a big bear hug and affirmed his love and acceptance of me.

The response I had feared never materialized. My parents could not have been more precious and supportive when faced with such a heart wrenching revelation. And they continue to be so to this day. The difficulty that I think both of them have had in the wake of all this has been reliving our early years as a family and asking themselves the unanswerable question, "What did we do wrong? Did we do something to cause this?"

If you've ever experienced the death of someone you love, you'll understand what I'm about to say. But in all of these conversations there was the initial listening and response and then after it all begins to really sink in, there is the shock phase. That can last a long time in some situations. God seems to have designed the human psyche so that when we are hit with devastating news of some kind, our bodies and emotions develop a protective covering which helps insulate us from just being totally leveled by bad news. God is good to us that way. Char experienced the shock. The kids did. My parents did. The church did.

I wish I could say that that was the worst of it and then it was over. But it wasn't. Because then (and I don't know how else to say this nicely) the shit really hit the fan.

 ELEVEN

FIFTEEN MINUTES OF FAME

YOU PROBABLY DON'T know this, but I'm a celebrity of sorts. Well, I guess that's not quite right. If you don't know it, then maybe we shouldn't call it celebrity status but my "fifteen minutes of fame" instead. Those are two very different things aren't they? One can make you famous, the other infamous.

My situation and resignation put the leadership of Grace Chapel in a very difficult position. The first order of business for them was to figure out how to manage the immediate crisis. The long-term ramifications of this decision would have to be dealt with as they arose, but for now, there was an unplanned, totally unexpected, out-of-the-blue resignation and for a sensational reason. Coming so closely on the heels of Haggard's resignation, there was a lot of concern as to what kind of media attention there might be.

That proved to be a very legitimate concern.

During the week before the Sunday announcement, the church hired a crisis management team. It was hoped that they would be able to come in and give guidance on how this situation should be handled, what should be said to the press, how calls should be responded to, what to expect. After hearing all the details and asking a lot of questions, they boiled down their responses to these:

1. There *will be* media coverage. There's no way to avoid it.

2. If some proactive action can be taken, the best case scenario would be a short article in the human interest/religion section of the paper, maybe a follow up article the next day and then it would blow over.

3. There exists the possibility of TV reporters, cameras and crews crawling all over the church campus and sitting in on a service and/or interviewing church members as they would come and go, and a strategy needs to be developed to handle that.

With that information a plan was developed. One of the members of the crisis team had a friend who was a reporter for one of the local newspapers. She contacted him and told him he could have exclusive rights to the story if he would wait until after Sunday evening to run it (so that our evening service could be done with). He came out to the church on Sunday afternoon, was shown the video, and from that developed his notes from which he would write his story.

Meanwhile, at my parent's home I had told them that they should be prepared for some media coverage, and explained everything. We had been advised to get out of town for a few days to avoid the media blitz that was expected. We went to bed that night not knowing what Monday morning's paper would bring. I woke up about 6:00 and walked out of the bedroom. My dad was already up sitting in the living room reading the paper and his first words to me were, "You made the front page." My heart sank and the baseball size knot in my stomach grew to the size of a basketball in less than a second.

I walked over, took the paper and read a front page story of my very personal and private life. I don't have the words to tell you how that impacted me. It was humiliating, and embarrassing. I felt de-humanized. Shamed. Victimized. Exposed to the world. We turned on the TV and there it was on the morning news as well. A reporter was standing outside the church commenting on the unfolding story and promising "more details as they become available."

Then, it grew even bigger.

Because of the fact that I was another evangelical pastor, from Colorado, and living just a few miles down the road from Ted Haggard, my resignation was perceived to be big time news. The reality is—I'm a small fish—there really was no reason this story needed to get the kind of attention it did. The AP wire picked up the story and it went out nationwide. A few weeks later in talking with one of the members of the crisis team, she informed me that within the first two weeks they had received over two hundred media requests for interviews. She said she could keep me busy for months doing interviews if I wanted to—newspapers, television stations, radio talk shows. The calls came in from *Inside Edition* on the west coast to ABC's *Nightline* on the east coast, and all sorts of places in-between.

I didn't see it personally, but I understand I even became a joke on SNL (*Saturday Night Live*). If I don't get this exactly right, please forgive me but it's close. The opening line said, "Another pastor in Colorado has come out and said he is gay." Then the joke was "Paul Barnes said he continually prayed and asked God to help him with his homosexuality. God answered by sending him hotter and hotter men." I just love comedic writers don't you? They sure know how to make me guffaw with laughter.

We stayed with my parents for three days and then spent another few days with our oldest daughter and her husband. When we finally headed home, it was with a lot of trepidation, not knowing what to expect. We actually timed our arrival home so that it would be under the cover of night. We pulled into the cul-de-sac, got into our garage and when we came into the house, the first thing I did, even before turning on the lights, was to go around and shut all the blinds. Then I ran downstairs, grabbed a roll of Christmas wrapping paper and covered up two sidelight windows that were on either side of our front door. We felt like prisoners in our own home. We did find out later that a news truck had camped outside our house while we were gone. We also heard that they had interviewed some of the neighbors. Fortunately, that turned out to be untrue. But it did create another issue that I'll address in a minute—how do we handle this with our neighbors?

We stayed secluded for the next number of days, unsure of what we might find if we ventured out. But for the most part what the crisis management team had said was accurate. Although they hadn't said anything about a front-page article, there was a follow-up article in Tuesday's paper, a very small one in Wednesday's paper, and then it was *kind of* over. Naturally there were articles in some smaller, neighborhood papers and the to-be-expected letters to the editors.

And then there was the Internet—the blogs, chat rooms, and websites.

I have yet to make up my mind as to how much of a blessing to the world the Internet is or if it's more of a curse. But there was a lot of internet activity with people writing all sorts of things. Some of it was supportive and understanding. Most of it was de-humanizing. The word "hypocrite" was thrown around an awful lot. "Got what he deserved." "Christianity is such a farce." When you read blogs and chat rooms one of the things you realize is there are a lot of cynical, angry people out there who love to spew their hatred over the Internet. It's a safe place to be mean but stay anonymous. In fact, to this day all you have to do is Google my name and you'll find a short, succinct article on me in Wikipedia. This is when I wish the Internet would just go away. But it all reminds me of something I read a while back. "No one is completely worthless. They can always be used as a bad example."

I mentioned a moment ago that because of the fact that a TV news truck camped outside our house, we realized that our neighbors might have been impacted in a personal and invasive way that they would certainly not have appreciated. We like our neighbors. For the most part, the same homeowners have lived in our cul-de-sac for fourteen years. Char and I felt awful that they might have been accosted by pushy reporters. We decided that we needed to get them all together and talk.

Shortly after coming back home, we invited them all over to the house saying that we wanted to get everyone together and discuss my situation. Everybody showed up. For that Char and I were glad. I began by telling them that I felt like there was a gigantic pink elephant sitting in the middle of our cul-de-sac and I didn't want us all to be constantly walking around it. So rather than pretending it wasn't there, I said let's look at it and see if we can't make it go away. Thus began yet another recounting of my story. Again, after it was all said and done, their responses were heartwarming. There were words of support and love and affirmation. There were hugs and offers of help. Flowers were sent. People invited us over. I don't know what kind of conversations went on in the privacy of their homes, but when with Char and me, they couldn't have been better neighbors to us. They continue to be so to this day, and I'm grateful for that. It's because of the way they responded that I don't see a pink elephant in our cul-de-sac any more and I don't think they do either.

I'm going to digress here a little, but let me address something. As I mentioned earlier, the word "hypocrite" was used a lot in reference to me. I hate that word so much. I hate what it means. I hate being labeled one. I hate the hypocrisy of those who call others hypocrites. I hate the fact that many skeptics in the world view the church as being full of them. It's a horrible word. Have I mentioned that I hate it?

I fully understand that when a person assumes a position of leadership in Christian ministry he or she is held to a higher standard of accountability and responsibility. A leader is called to be an example, a model to others. That goes with the territory. And there are standards that a leader is expected to maintain in order to remain a leader in the Christian community.

However, I have always been bothered by the way we rank and categorize sin as Christians. Please understand, this is not my attempt to justify my sin, and if you take it as such, you will have misunderstood everything I'm trying to say. I am talking about a much bigger issue here than just my personal struggle. My basic understanding of how God views sin is that sin is sin. There is no one sin that is greater than any other. All sin is equally disturbing to God. However, it is also true that some sins have greater ramifications than others: to us, our families and loved ones, and the greater community in which we live.

But greater ramifications do not equate to a greater sin in God's eyes. Sin is sin.

Yet we humans don't seem to live by that fundamental principle. People love to rank sin. Sure, our lists differ from one person to the next, but people naturally have a pecking order of what they think are the "not-so-bad" sins and the "gross, horrible sins."

I think part of it has to do with the pride factor we all live with. It makes us feel better when we think other people are lower down on the "sin-scale" that we are. I also think it has to do with our basic approach to spiritual maturity. This is the much bigger issue. We operate on the premise that a spiritually mature person is one who has his or her act together, so he or she should have conquered sin and figured out how to gain victory over it. That paradigm is radically different from the idea that spiritual maturity is not an end product but rather a process. It's a process that recognizes that *everyone* (leaders included) is on a journey with God, who in His own time and His own way woos us back to greater fascination and preoccupation with Him rather than the unhealthy focus that we have on the things in our outer world.

I've noticed the hypocrisy we live with and it's been something that has bothered me for years. For example, there are so many pastors who run their church as if it were their own personal empire. In fact there are colleges that teach budding pastors this kind of leadership model. These men are authoritative and dictatorial. They drive members out of their congregation if those members question decisions or direction. The board is frequently a group of "yes-men" who basically rubber-stamp the plans of the pastor. Often there is little financial accountability.

I was channel surfing just last night and landed on a Christian station which had a twenty-something pastor on. He was the grandson of a well-known but not very well respected pastor and evangelist. His father was also a preacher. Well, the grandson was preaching at church this particular day and he was giving the devil fits. At one point he said, "When my grandfather dies and my father dies, I'm taking over this place." And then he pointed his finger to the ground and said, "So devil, you're going to be dealing with us for a long time to come." That was all I could stand. I surfed on to another channel and began watching a movie. The pastor's comments were arrogant, braggadocio, and disgusting.

As I understand the New Testament, this kind of self-important, haughty leadership model is totally at odds with the servant-leadership principles that Jesus told His followers to live by. "If anyone wants to be first, he must be the very last, and the servant of all."[45] "Everyone who exalts himself will be humbled, and he who humbles himself will be exalted."[46] Yet these little empire builders are allowed to continue running their empire. They don't have to resign. I mean after all, their leadership style isn't a moral issue. Or is it?

Let me give you another example. I marvel at certain pastors you'll see on their weekly television shows who are horribly obese. It's obvious they can't control their appetite. You never hear them preaching a sermon on gluttony. Yet I read in scripture, "Put a knife to your throat if you are given to gluttony."[47] Next to pride and envy, gluttony is third on the list of the seven deadly sins. This is a dirty little secret for a large number of Christians and just about every church in America. It seems that certain Christians are very quick to label smoking, drinking, and gambling as sins but for some reason gluttony is accepted and tolerated. An obese pastor is allowed to keep his job. I mean after all, gluttony is not a moral issue. Or is it?

I could give you other examples, but hopefully you're getting my point. This whole thing about the way we categorize and rank sin—something is not right about that. Do you know what happens when we do that? It drives sin underground. People who struggle with the "gross, horrible sins" don't feel the liberty to say, "I struggle" because they know they will be judged, condemned, and kicked out of the church. As the gentleman in the e-mail said to me, "The church is the only army in the world that shoots its wounded." I agree. Why do we do that? Can we as followers of Jesus Christ not come up with a more redemptive way of dealing with broken, hurting people? Can we not figure out a way to take the things that are negatives in our fallen human condition and make them positives?

I say all of this just to try and help us realize that things are not always as black and white as we like to think they are. Life is lived in multiple shades of gray. This whole issue speaks to the point of the church being a redemptive community rather than a rejecting one. I love the church. It was my life for thirty years. But this is one thing that is horribly wrong with the church. Now, fortunately, there is a growing group of thoughtful Christ-followers who share my frustration. It was evidenced by some of the letters we received after my resignation.

Let me share a few of them with you.

"I am 64 and have known the Lord for 55 years. Through many trials I have learned that God is a "BIG" God. He never fails us. Through bad or good He is always there to forgive. Sin is sin. There is no degree of sin. He died on the cross for all sins. We as humans seem to think one sin is worse than others…there is nothing too big for Him to handle. Lean on His everlasting arms and remember Matthew 19:26, 'With man this is impossible, but with God all things are possible.'"

———————————

"When we think of all the other options that the elder board had in dealing with this situation at Grace, we really wonder whether they did the right thing. For Grace Chapel, we hope so, but for you, it doesn't seem like it. It pains us greatly to see you suffering. It seems very ironic and cruel that the church you founded that has extended Christian love and acceptance to those struggling with all sorts of personal confusion and sin now seems unable to extend the same love and acceptance to you…we are all sinners trying to find our way in this world, and we all share your pain and the joy of knowing that Christ took our sins with Him to the cross."

———————————

"I have no clue what your struggle must have been like over the years. But I do know the personal struggles I've had and how I, too, have beaten myself up as well. You've heard it said that we all face our own dragons, and you're quite correct when you say or intimate the condemnation of the villagers when they become familiar with a certain variety of those dragons. With God there is no rank regarding sin. When will the church get on board? Do we really understand the overwhelming love Christ had for the woman caught in adultery? Unfortunately, the statistics prove not. Consequences, yes…condemnation, no! The kind of dragon you fight, Paul makes no difference to me. The only difference in my dragon is of its color…"

"I can't even imagine what Pastor Paul and Char are going through. I'm also in shock that he wasn't asked to stay—I know there are rules and doctrine for a church. I just don't understand where is the compassion and love and forgiveness in the rules. As Pastor Paul discussed several weeks ago—we are all sinners, some conquer that sin and it's gone; and some struggle with sin every day of their lives. Sometimes we sin, we regret, we suffer, we ask for forgiveness and it's hard to believe that Jesus would forgive us. But He has already forgiven us and it doesn't matter what that sin is. It just doesn't matter...I don't understand a church that will dispose of a gifted, loving Pastor who built a church with his blood, sweat and tears by asking him to leave or accepting his resignation. Why not swallow the pride and bow our heads with humility and embrace him for admitting his struggle? And love him through this no matter how long or hard the road is for him. If we were all to be judged by the 'church' how many gossips, convicts, murderers, drug addicts, alcoholics, adulterers, shopaholics, jealous, greedy, selfish, envious people sitting among us would not be able to attend?"

In many ways, I hesitated sharing some of these because I don't want anyone to think poorly of Grace Chapel or the leaders of Grace. I love Grace Chapel. It was my life's work. I love, admire, and respect the men that served as fellow elders with me. As I said at the beginning of this chapter, my situation and sudden resignation put them in a very difficult position. When I speak of the fact that the church is the only army that shoots its wounded or the church needs to think through how to be a more redemptive rather than rejecting community, I'm not talking about Grace Chapel specifically.

I'm talking about the church at large...

the great big Body of Christ on this earth

composed of many churches and many
denominations…

but all filled with people who are…

gossips,

convicts,

murderers,

drug addicts,

alcoholics,

adulterers,

shopaholics,

jealous,

greedy,

selfish,

envious,

like me…a struggler.

Where does a struggler like me go?

---

[45] Mark 9:35

[46] Luke 18:14

[47] Proverbs 23:2

REFLECTION #3
THE GREAT DIVIDE

I've always thought the name Caleb was a great name. It has a Hebrew origin and it means "faithful" or "bold." Those are characteristics I'd like to have in my life. I first met Caleb when he came to one of our Sunday evening services. One of the things we were doing as a church was attempting to reach the lost generation, the emergents. Those teens and twenty-something young adults who have basically abandoned the church because they view it as irrelevant and feel disenfranchised from it. We had a service geared for them called Elevation. We were attempting to make it a place where genuine community could happen and where people could come and find acceptance and hope. And it was working.

One Sunday evening about 5:15, a tall, slender, dark haired young man in his late twenties came into the sanctuary and sat down on the back row. I'd never seen him before and since the service didn't start until 6:00 and most people who regularly came usually didn't show up until about twenty minutes after six, I knew this had to be his first time. I went over and introduced myself and we began talking.

It turned out Caleb had recently moved into the area. He'd been helping lead worship in the church he'd been involved in previously. He had started helping lead worship in the church he was now going to as well. I asked him where he went and his comment was, "I attend MCC." That's all he said. For the uninitiated, that might need to be followed up with the question, "What is MCC?" But I knew. MCC is the Metropolitan Community Church. It is a world-wide association of churches for gay, lesbian, and transgender people. While many have no interest in spiritual things and some have an actual disgust for organized religion, there are gay men and women who have a spiritual orientation. Spiritual longings are not just reserved for the heterosexual. There are those in the gay community who want to grow in their relationship with God and figure out how to live their lives based on a spiritual foundation.

I asked Caleb why he had come to visit us and his answer made me laugh. The purpose for his visit was because he had heard about the music we were doing at Elevation. One thing that is an ongoing battle in the Christian community is the issue of music. It is amazing to me how people can get so up tight and bothered by different music styles and preferences. This issue has caused more church splits, more upset people, and more individuals leaving one church to attend another than you can shake a stick at. It's silly really. I wish folks could get as excited and passionate about the things that really matter as they do about their music, but after thirty years of working in the church, I learned a long time ago that's just the nature of the beast, and it's not going to change.

Well, it turned out that a number of people at MCC were unhappy with the kind of music they were experiencing in their church service. Apparently it was very traditional. They sang a lot of hymns. They didn't use many instruments and there was a growing segment of people who wanted some more contemporary stuff thrown into the mix. Get some guitars and drums in there and spice things up a bit. That was the comment that made me laugh, because when he said that my first thought was, "This is amazing. It doesn't matter who you are or where you go to church, people are people." They were having the same issue in their church as we were in ours. Ahh...maybe I'd finally found at least *one* point of common ground!

I knew there was a story with Caleb and I wanted to find out what it was. So over the next six months or so we would meet for coffee somewhat regularly and I had a chance to get into his life a little bit. The first time we sat down together, one of the first things he said to me was, "I know I wouldn't be accepted in a church like yours." It broke my heart. Although he didn't really know that much about our church, *intuitively* he sensed that it would be a place where he probably wouldn't be very welcomed. And intuitively, I knew he was right. That formed the basis for our first very heart to heart conversation.

It's interesting to me that during the time Caleb and I were meeting, I never shared anything with him about my struggle. Even with a fellow Christian who was openly gay, I didn't feel safe. Instead, I asked a lot of questions and listened intently and inside I wept for Caleb. He had grown up in a very conservative Christian home. His father, in fact, was a pastor. When he came out in his late teens he was disowned by his family and subsequently his life spiraled out of control. He started smoking, got involved with drugs, and began to drink heavily. It's so sad what we do when we are rejected by the people we love—we turn to all sorts of things just to try and deaden the pain. At the time our paths crossed Caleb was still in process. He was getting to a point of acceptance about who he was and how his family felt about him. He was developing a good support system of friends and was actively seeking to be productive with his life.

I realize the comments I'm about to make are not going to make me very popular. This is not the kind of chapter you would find in *How to Win Friends and Influence People*. The reason is that the two groups of people I most identify with will probably not want to identify with me once I'm through sharing some of my thoughts.

I strongly identify with the Christian community. At the age of seventeen I had a very profound, life changing experience when I encountered Jesus Christ. That is something that no one can take away from me. In the years that followed, going to a Christian college, on to Seminary, and then spending almost 30 years working in the church, my life mission and goal has been to try and help people realize how much God loves them and wants to be involved in helping them live a life of purpose and fulfillment.

Even if there was no benefit to be found in Christianity other than simply following the teachings of Jesus, that would be worth it to me. I don't know of another teacher or teaching, philosophy or religion, either past or present that would be as worthy of trying to follow as are the teachings of Jesus Christ. What He taught was profound. And seeking to live by those teachings can be tremendously life-enriching. But then to have a personal encounter with Him—that is even more deeply transforming.

That's why I have such a hard time understanding these people who call themselves Christians, yet they are traveling around the country protesting against homosexuals, picketing, and waving placards that say "Fags burn in hell" and "God hates homos." What do they think they are accomplishing by this kind of behavior, and how in the world can they possibly think that they are being accurate representatives of Jesus Christ? I mentioned earlier the phrase, "We've got to hate the sin, but love the sinner" that people in the church use so frequently. It's tragic because that statement *horribly* oversimplifies how Christians are to relate to those around them. Even worse, my observation has been that many people who throw that saying around don't seem to know exactly how to effectively practice both hate and love at the same time. Can *that* even be done? It seems very challenging to figure out how to lovingly hate or hatefully love.

I also identify with the gay community. My struggle with my sexuality is not an isolated one. If people think that the men and women who ultimately embrace their sexual orientation do so with joy and frivolity—those people are fools. The road to accepting the challenge of one's sexuality is a very long and hard one to walk. It is a road filled with misunderstanding, self-loathing, confusion, and angst. It involves hard conversations with loved ones. It is a road filled with a lot of tears, self-doubting, sadness, uncertainty, despair, and often rejection. It is *not* an easy road to walk, but rather it's like walking barefoot down a path that is covered with broken glass. Somewhere along the way, to some degree or another, some sense of acceptance develops, and the issues get "semi-resolved," although there is often heartache and pain that lasts a lifetime.

I was watching a documentary a while back on how homosexuals were treated during WWII by the Nazis. It was terrible. The hatred, persecution, and mistreatment they experienced were horrific. But the thing that struck me most was listening to the men who were being interviewed. The six or seven men that shared their experiences were now all in their 70s and 80s, and yet tears still came to their eyes and their voices quivered as they talked about something they had experienced fifty years earlier. It made me realize there is often pain in the heart that can stay there for a lifetime. Of course, many of their friends suffered the same fate as did over six million Jews and other undesirables. Yet those who made it out alive have spent a lifetime living with the consequences of other people's prejudices and ignorance.

I also have just as hard a time understanding some people in the gay community. I learned a long time ago that there are some very evil people in the gay world. Individuals who love to "out" others, who take pleasure in ruining another person's life, destroying their career, their family, all in the name of some higher cause they think they are advancing. That's what someone was planning to do to me. It's very difficult for me to understand how a person can be that heartless. Yet they're out there.

In *any* group of people in society, there will be individuals who live, behave and believe, extremely. Even for their own group, they are not mainstream—they are extreme. While you will always find those fringe people in every group, they don't represent the majority. To judge an entire group by the behavior and words of the extremists—that's wrong.

Here's what that means practically. It's not an accurate assessment for men and women in the Christian community to think that all gay people are out to destroy the family in America and are seeking to push some kind of social revolution. I have real sympathy with the individuals who have the bumper sticker on their car that says, "Focus on your own damn family." The reality is most gay men and women have the same hopes, dreams, and ambitions as everyone else. They want to be in a loving relationship. They long for quality friendships. They have responsible jobs. They volunteer in their communities. They desire to be productive members of society.

It's also not right for people in the gay community to think that all Christians are religious bigots who are the cancer of society and need to be zapped into oblivion. I know, because of the letters and e-mails I've received that many, many Christians have had to wrestle with this issue on a very personal level. They've had a loved one—a son, a daughter, a sister, a brother, a parent who has struggled with their sexuality and as Christians they have had many sleepless nights and shed a lot tears as they have tried to understand all of the complexities surrounding homosexuality. Yet most finally come to a point where they begin to relate with some sense of understanding, acceptance and love to those in their circle of relationships who've come out.

Other than the issue of music styles, is it not possible for us to find some kind of common ground of understanding with each other? Is the divide so great that it can't be bridged? Are the prejudices and misunderstandings on *both* sides so deeply ingrained in us that we're unable (or maybe it's that we're unwilling) to let go of them? If you want to know what my tension is, it's this: I identify with both the Christian community and the gay community. Yet I am disgusted and ashamed by the extremists in both groups as well.

As I wrap up this chapter, I'm sitting here at my computer shaking my head. Writing these words has made me very sad. But I will end where I began. With Caleb. I enjoyed my times with him. I enjoyed *him*. He was thoughtful. Spiritual. Conflicted. He was on a journey of self-discovery and he was on a journey with God. I eventually lost contact with him, but the thing that still makes me sad to this day is that Caleb never did come back to our church. Intuitively he knew that it wasn't a place for a person like him. Where does a struggler like Caleb go?

REFLECTION #4
TO *ALL* MY FELLOW STRUGGLERS

When my story became national news I began to get cards and emails from people all over the country. I was surprised at the volume and the content of all this correspondence. It seemed that suddenly people everywhere wanted to communicate with me and tell me their story, offer their insights, affirm their love, let me know their thoughts were with me, and in general empathize with me. There was not a single email, letter, or card that was nasty or negative. Not one. And I received well over 1,000 messages. It was unexpected. It was heartbreaking. It also confirmed something I already knew: many, many people struggle with homosexuality.

I have a tendency to think big picture. Here is an instance of how that plays itself out. There are two very different perspectives on the number of people in our society who have a same sex orientation. Gay rights activists have long said that 10 percent of our population is gay. Evangelical Christian leaders have long disputed that figure, saying it is grossly over exaggerated and that in reality the number is probably no more than two to three percent.

For the sake of argument, let's use the three percent number. If there are 300,000,000 Americans that means there are 9,000,000 people in our society for whom sexual orientation is an issue. Nine million people are a lot of people. That's the entire population of New York City, plus about another million. Also in our society there are 70,000,000 people who claim to be evangelical Christians. Three percent of 70,000,000 is 2.1 million. Since the church is reflective of society in so many ways, I do not think there is any reason to assume that that number would be significantly smaller in the evangelical community.

Conceivably, that means there are 2.1 million *evangelical* Christians struggling with a same sex orientation. Where are all those people? In hiding. They sit next to you each Sunday in your church. They eat with you at your fellowship dinners. They teach your children in Sunday school. They serve as leaders on your boards and committees. They join you on your mission trips. They attend Bible studies in your homes. But because of the nature of our church culture, they stay hidden, condemned to suffer in silence, ashamed and afraid knowing that if their secret ever becomes known, they will face horrible consequences.

Let me give you a small sampling of the messages people sent me. Here's a portion of a two page letter I received:

"Dearest Brother and Friend: I must have composed some version of this note in my mind over the past 24 hours or so, looking forward to the day that I would actually sit down and commit my thoughts to paper. I wish I could hand deliver this letter to you—only to embrace you as a friend and brother. I want you to know how freeing this letter will be for me and that it has taken your grand example of bravery and honor to write it. I want to come out and just explain the nature of this letter. I too struggle with homosexuality. I really can't accurately pinpoint when and where these feelings started, however, they've been there for as long as I can remember, and I've had to carry them throughout my life thus far. Because of the environment of our society and churches, I have been forced to compartmentalize my feelings and continue through this life without anyone to really talk to. I wrestle almost daily with my feelings, and have cried myself to sleep countless times pleading with God to make me 'normal.' I have never felt safe enough, even among my friends and family to divulge these details, and I remain scared even to this day. I, just like you, died before I had the chance to live, and for that I grieve. My only hope is that our most glorious Lord will be able to resurrect a more perfected life in me (and you), and that we will be able to glorify Him through this."

And then there was this e-mail: "I know you are going to get a ton of e-mails but I have had a burning question for years that I feel maybe you can answer for me. It's about the combination of Christianity and homosexuality. My best friend on this planet is both a Christian and a homosexual. I have known him for 13 or 14 years and even though we have never spoken about his homosexuality I know he has had a very tormented life trying to deal with the combination of the two."

And this one: "Having lost a cousin to AIDS and another cousin's son is near death due to this disease, I have questioned the source of homosexuality in our family. I do believe that some choose it as a lifestyle, but many more have no control over it. Needless to say, this is an area that I don't have the answer, but I continue to have questions."

And this one: "There is not one person who does not have a friend or a loved one that struggles with homosexuality. My own brother has struggled with it since he was a young boy. I have watched him suffer with guilt and pain being brought up in the Christian community...and I have also seen God's GRACE and hand in it all."

And this one: "I am a 60-year-old layman in my church who has struggled with homosexuality all my life...For some reason I feel impressed to ask if you would be willing to let me come and pray with you. I don't claim to have 'the cure' or any such thing. I only know that I empathize..."

A particular website generated a number of comments. I'll just share one. A young man wrote in and said, "For a couple of years now I have been attracted to men. I have been raised Mormon all my life, and I have been taught that these things are wrong…It is a constant battle to fight the feelings I am having and what I have been taught all my life. Has anyone else gone through this? What did you do?"

One individual responded, "I understand the feelings you're going through. I am a Christian and there was a period of my life where I struggled with my faith and sexuality too. In fact, I was fairly involved in the 'ex-gay' community. During that time in my life, I felt strong in my faith, but completely alone and hopeless…to the point of just wanting to die. I have learned that I am not condemned by my life choices any longer, because I chose His gift to me of saving me from EVERYTHING that I could ever do to myself here in this lifetime. God's love is NOT conditional. It is not bound by OUR human standards. He loves each of us REGARDLESS of ourselves. We are ALL (Gay, str8, whatever!) in the same mess here on earth and only He can save us from ourselves. Nothing more, nothing less. So, whether it is right or wrong is not the question. The question is, have you accepted the gift He has offered to you which extinguishes any and ALL the 'wrong' that needs to be eliminated in your life? John 3:16 & 17 'For God so loved the world that he gave his one and only Son, that WHOEVER believes in him shall not perish but have eternal life. FOR GOD DID NOT SEND HIS SON INTO THE WORLD TO CONDEMN THE WORLD, BUT TO SAVE THE WORLD THROUGH HIM.' That's what it's about! It's not about condemnation, but about salvation."

As I read and reread all the correspondence that I received I shed a lot of tears. So many, so many that are tormented, that struggle with guilt and shame. I thought, what can I say to them? Then I realized that really anything I might say would be shallow and seem empty compared to what God might say to them.

So, here are some words from a book called *True Faced*.[48] They are words that come from the heart of God to each and every person on this planet that needs to hear the Voice of Love pouring into their life.

"What if I tell them who they are?

What if I take away any element of fear in condemnation, judgment or rejection?

What if I tell them I love them, will always love them? That I love them right now, no matter what they've done, as much as I love my only son? That there's nothing they can do to make my love go away?

What if I tell them there are no lists?

What if I tell them I don't keep a log of past offenses, of how little they pray, how often they've let me down, made promises they don't keep?

What if I tell them they are righteous, with my righteousness right now?

What if I tell them they can stop beating themselves up, they can stop being so formal, stiff and jumpy around me?

What if I tell them I'm crazy about them?

What if I tell them, even if they run to the ends of the earth and do the most horrible unthinkable things, that when they come back, I'd receive them with tears and a party?

What if I tell them that I am their savior and that they're going to heaven no matter what – it's a done deal?

What if I tell them they have a new nature—saints, not saved sinners who should not 'buck-up and be better if they were any kind of Christians, after all He's done for you!'

What if I tell them I actually live in them now? That I've put my love, power and nature inside of them, at their disposal?

What if I tell them they don't have to put on a mask? That it is ok to be who they are that this moment, with all their junk. That they don't need to pretend about how close we are, how much they pray or don't, how much Bible they read or don't.

What if they knew they didn't have to look over their shoulder for fear if things get too good, the other shoe is going to drop?

What if they knew I will never, ever use the word punish in relationship to them?

What if they knew that when they mess up, I will never 'get back' at them?

What if they were convinced that bad circumstances aren't my way of evening the score for taking advantage of me?

What if they knew the basis of our friendship isn't how little they sin, but how much they let me love them?

What if I tell them they can hurt my heart, but that I will never hurt theirs?

What if I tell them it isn't about their self-effort, but allowing me to live my life through them?"

At this juncture, I *do* want to write something to my fellow strugglers—hopefully without sounding patronizing. I understand the difficult road you have had to walk.

No doubt there have been many times when your journey has seemed so hard, exhausting, and lonely. You may have had to deal with the pain of family rejection, loss of friends, discrimination on the job, hateful comments, Christian intolerance, and a whole host of other demeaning, demoralizing, and isolating experiences. Perhaps you've spent a lifetime, as I have, wearing masks because of the fear of what might happen if those masks are removed.

For me, it's those times when faith becomes such a source of strength. To choose to believe that God *does* care deeply about me; that He completely understands the hurt in my life, and the longing I have for love and acceptance. When I read those words from *True Faced* and really let them sink in, I *feel* a whole lot better. I begin to *think* differently about myself and about Him. Because regardless of what people may think, how they may respond, and what they might say, it's a source of strength and comfort knowing that God loves me and that He will always love me. It's a source of hope knowing that there is nothing I can do to make Him stop loving me and in spite of my struggle, it brings security to my life knowing that God is crazy about me. May those thoughts strengthen and comfort you as well.

"When I said, 'My foot is slipping,' your love, O Lord, supported me. When anxiety was great within me, your consolation brought joy to my soul.'"[49]

---

[48] *True Faced*, Bill Thrall, Bruce McNichol, John Lynch, Navpress, Copyright © 2003

[49] Psalm 94:18-19

REFLECTION #5

THE LABRADOODLE

Char and I have two very precious girls. Both are married and have terrific husbands whom we love dearly. Our oldest daughter Ashley has been married for a few years and about nine months after her wedding she called one day. She had been online looking for a dog. For some strange reason she thought it would be nice for them, as a newly married couple, to have a dog. So the search began. Her call was to inform us that she'd found one. It was called a Labradoodle. Now, first of all it took me forever to learn how to pronounce it. Second, I had no idea what the thing looked like. It was a cross between a Labrador Retriever and a Poodle.

Have you ever seen those commercials where two very different things are put together and at the end the announcer says, "That's not natural." When I heard about the Labradoodle that was one of the first thoughts I had. Who in their right mind would start messing with Mother Nature and try to breed a Labrador Retriever with a Poodle? It's just not natural.

But the decision was made, so one day Ashley, Tiffany (our other daughter), and Char took off in the car to head for central Nebraska where they were to meet up with the breeder of this alien creature and bring it back to its new home.

When Char got home later that day she had a bit of a hard time describing "Jake" to me.

"Awkward in size with long legs, kind of a cute face, curly hair all over his body, sweet," she said.

We looked at each other and remarked, "We sure hope Ashley knows what she's gotten herself in to."

Less than 24 hours later the first of many phone calls came. "I think I've made a mistake!" Ashley said on the other end of the line. "Jake isn't bonding with me. He won't come when I call. He's peed in the house…"

Well, you can imagine the direction that conversation took.

Sadly for Jake, his days at Matt and Ashley's house were numbered. He began to be passed around from one house to another as people kept him for a few days and then decided they didn't want him. I think it was five different homes he went through. Now before you dog lovers start getting too agitated, there is a happy ending to Jake's story. He finally landed in a good home, so rest easy. He is now a very happy and contented Labradoodle.

I finally got my first glimpse of Jake when he came to stay at our house for a few days. We became kind of a halfway house for dogs. Honestly, he wasn't much to look at. The minute I saw him, I thought again, "That's not natural." Some things are just better left alone, don't you think?

Jake comes to mind sometimes when I think about the church. In *theory* the church should be a place where people, regardless of background or color, social standing, education or material possessions, can come together and be a community. The church should be a place where all those societal barriers are broken down. "My prayer is not for them alone. I pray also for those who will believe in me through their message, that all of them may be one, Father, just as you are in me and I am in you. May they also be in us so that the world may believe that you have sent me. I have given them the glory that you gave me, that they may be one as we are one: I in them and you in me. May they be brought to complete unity to let the world know that you sent me and have loved them even as you have loved me."[50]

In theory it should also be a place where people—broken people and people who don't yet know they're broken—can come together and be there for each other. "Love each other as I have loved you."[2] The broken people would have help in learning how to live life effectively, sometimes in the midst of their brokenness and sometimes by experiencing release from their brokenness. And the people who don't know they're broken could come to realize that in reality they really are and they can begin to empathize with the brokenness of others and also begin to look a little more deeply within themselves to see what dark things are lurking in the recesses of their minds and hearts. At least in my mind, that's the way it *should* be.

Sadly, it doesn't often work that way. What seems to happen when the broken and the unbroken try to come together is you end up getting spiritual Labradoodles. It's not natural. The broken don't feel accepted, understood, embraced and cared for. The unbroken feel smugly above the broken, sad for the condition of their brothers and sisters but glad nonetheless that they aren't in such a state. Even though in theory, I know what the church should be, sometimes I wonder if in trying to have it become so, we end up producing these unnatural spiritual Labradoodles. Maybe the unbroken should just stay with their own kind. You know, the *I'm O.K., You're O.K.* crowd. That way they could stay in a perpetual state of delusion. And maybe the broken need to just hang out with other broken people. That way they would at least fulfill the old adage that "misery loves company." At least then, both groups would be hanging out with their own kind and everyone would probably feel somewhat understood, accepted, and loved.

But something inside of me deeply rebels at that thought. Because when everything is said and done, *that* is what's not natural. As ungainly and unsightly and ugly (I'm sorry Jake) as that Labradoodle was, *the* place on this planet for all the spiritual Labradoodles to hang out and find love and acceptance regardless of their inner or outer ugliness *should be the church.* Since *everybody* is broken (whether everyone realizes it yet or not), the church should be the place where *everyone* can experience the redemptive grace of God and find whatever healing He may have for them.

Again, I deeply appreciate some words from *True Faced* on this subject. They are words that reflect what the church should strive to become.

> "A grace-filled community gives us the grace needed to resolve our sin, not hide it. In a grace-filled community, a different view of life in God biases the whole culture toward repentance. For starters, this community expects and anticipates imperfections. Yes, we honor others in the community as saints, but we also face the reality of each other's sin. We applaud vulnerability and view godliness as something much more than the presence of good behavior and the absence of bad behavior. We're too busy dancing to hold on to that dead weight. The individuals in this community trust God to mature them from the inside out, by the power of His Spirit…in His timing. No one feels a need to hide, for no one's parading his or her own righteousness. Everyone feels safe to be real and alive."[52]

Ken Medema is a Christian composer, singer and songwriter who was born almost blind. His eyes let him tell light from shadow and see the outlines of major objects. Much of his music focuses on topics like justice, hunger, poverty, the homeless, and previously unaccepted people. In 2006 he released a double CD entitled, *25 to Life.* One of the songs is entitled, "If This Is Not the Place." The words of this song reflect the heart cry of a spiritual Labradoodle.

"If this is not a place, where tears are understood, then where shall I go to cry?

And if this is not a place, where my spirit can take wings, then where shall I go to fly?

I don't need another place, for trying to impress you, with just how good and virtuous I am. No, no, no, I don't need another place, for always being on top of things. Everybody knows that it's a sham, it's a sham.

I don't need another place, for always wearing smiles, even when it's not the way I feel. I don't need another place, to mouth the same old platitudes; everybody knows that it's not real.

So if this is not a place where my questions can be asked, then where shall I go to seek?

And if this is not a place, where my heart cry can be heard, where, tell me where, shall I go to speak? So if this is not a place, where tears are understood, where shall I go, where shall I go to fly?"

That is the kind of place the church should seek to be, don't you think?

---

[50] John 17:20-23
[51] John 15:12
[52] *True Faced*, p.161

 TWELVE

THE OFFICE

I HATE WINTER. I KNOW hate is a strong word and should be reserved for only a few things in life. It's one of those words that should be used very sparingly, if at all. But, when it comes to my feelings about winter, hate is a word I feel justified in using. It sounds funny coming from a guy who has lived most of his life in Colorado. Aren't we supposed to *love* winter? In fact, one of the first questions people frequently ask when they find out where I'm from is, "Oh, do you ski?" My simple, one word answer always seems to perplex them. "No." I can tell from the look on their face that a guy from Colorado who doesn't ski is as much of a paradox as someone from California who doesn't surf, or someone living in Arizona who doesn't golf. It just doesn't compute. But I hate winter. I don't like being cold. I don't like snow. Give me the nice warm sun, a palm tree, and some beautiful Caribbean blue water and I'm a *very* happy camper.

I love seeing the mountains from a distance (we have a beautiful view of the mountains from our house…very inspiring) but I start getting claustrophobic when I get *into* the mountains, and to be in snow and be cold—those are two things that just aren't to my liking. You can't keep your car clean (and I get anal about keeping my car clean). Your garage gets filthy, you track gunk into the house, your hands chap, the skin on your fingers split, and you can't wear shorts and flip flops (one of my preferred ways of dressing).

I guess one of the biggest reasons I don't like winter is because it depresses me. My spirit gets heavier in winter with its long, dark nights and the grayness of the sky when it's snowing. Char *loves* winter. She's the optimist in our family. She likes it when it snows and the world seems to slow down. I will have to admit that it's nice when you have a meeting planned at night and it starts snowing and the meeting is cancelled and you get to stay snuggled nice and warm in your house, sitting by a fire. Unexpected nights off because of bad weather are kind of special. I doubt if they've ever cancelled a meeting in Phoenix because of bad weather. But even here in Colorado, we don't have that many times when the weather shuts things down.

I've jokingly said that I absolutely love the spring, summer, and fall in Colorado—it's the other nine months of the year I can't stand! But in all fairness to my state, most of the time we have beautiful winters—really we do. We get a tremendous amount of sunshine. There are quick little snow storms that blow through the area and then melt within the next day or two. But, occasionally we'll have one of those hundred year storms—we've had about a dozen of them in the last twenty years. That's when I really go nuts.

This winter was one of those years. Seven weekends in a row, starting right before Christmas—count 'em—*seven* weekends in a row we had gotten dumped on with snow. And I don't mean just a little dusting. The snow kept coming, and coming and coming. We were shoveling over and over again. The mound of snow by our driveway was above our heads. It's really hard to throw snow that high, so then it starts creeping into the driveway. The pile of snow in the middle of our cul-de-sac was at least ten feet high. And you have to understand I'm not prone to exaggeration—seriously this was a nightmare of a winter, especially for a guy who hates snow. It's that global warming thing. Because while we were getting dumped on in Denver, they were playing golf in Chicago and the lakes weren't freezing in Minnesota, so they couldn't do their traditional ice fishing. The weather was messed up all over the place. I blame it all on global warming.

It was in the pre-dawn darkness of a cold, snowy Saturday morning that I headed over to the office to pack up the last remaining shelves of books, miscellaneous stuff from my desk drawers, and final few drawers in my filing cabinets. I determined to make quick work of it. It was depressing being there. The darkness outside, and the snow, was reflective of how I was feeling on the inside. In fact, over the previous number of weeks, it had been really difficult for me to even think about packing up my office. For one thing it seemed overwhelming (I had thousands of books on my shelves and twenty-eight years of accumulated files, mementos, and basically a lot of junk stuffed in drawers and cabinets). It was difficult to even think about. And there was a part of me, a deeper part that was resisting it, because in a very tangible way it represented the finality of the whole situation. I guess I wasn't emotionally ready to accept that.

Char and I went over one night after the office was closed and tried to make a little headway with it. It was so overwhelming we left. Then she and a friend went over another day and really made a dent in packing up a lot of my books, getting them ready for storage. I appreciated that a lot. I was supposed to go with them, but emotionally I just couldn't do it. Then finally, on that cold, snowy Saturday about 5:30 in the morning, I headed over to finish the job.

I wonder how many of you have had to clear out your desk because you were fired, you quit, or a better job opportunity came along. Regardless of the reason, you became part of the "clean-out-your-desk club." Not ever having done it before I realized it's not a club I like being a member of. I quickly packed up the last remaining books, took down pictures and knick-knacks off the shelves, throwing everything into the car as quickly as I could. I wanted to stay there as short a time as possible. It worked. I got it done, put the last box in the car went back into the office, took one final look around and then all that had happened hit me hard, and I started to cry. I sat on the edge of the desk looking around at that empty, hollow office. The only things that remained were the filing cabinets, lots of dusty shelves, a few fake plants and junk that would be thrown away. And I cried. No, I sobbed. In so many ways, it represented the end of a life, at least the end of my life as I had known it. Twenty eight years of blood, sweat and tears—my life's work. Gone. And I wept for what was lost and how it had been lost.

I grabbed a Kleenex, wiped my eyes and headed to the door to shut the light off when suddenly one last picture caught my eye. I'd almost forgotten it. It was one of my favorite pictures that had been hanging above the door. It was a picture of Jesus—just His face with His nailed pierced hand gently wrapped around a little lamb. The only part of the lamb you could see was its face. The reason I love the picture so much is because of the expression on the little lamb's face. He looks so contented. The little guy is so peaceful and at rest. He almost has a slight smile on his face as he is being gently embraced and held close to Jesus. I like that. It's the place I wanted to be, especially right then at that moment in time—content in His arms, wanting for nothing, being held securely, knowing that everything was going to be all right. The picture reminded me of all that, and that's why I love it so much.

I took it down off the wall, tucked it under my arm, shut the light off and opened the door. A frigid blast of wind took my breath as I locked the door behind me. And I realized with a stabbing pain in my heart that it was snowing even harder.

 THIRTEEN

THE FOG

I WOKE UP THIS MORNING to one of the densest fogs I've seen in a long time. As I made my way in the pre-dawn darkness over to the gym I found myself creeping along at ten miles per hour trying to see just a few feet in front of the car. They reported on the radio that in some parts of town visibility was only a quarter of a mile and in other parts it was zero. I was in zero land.

I don't know if you've ever seen it, but back in 1980 John Carpenter released a movie called *The Fog*. In it, dead sailors pay a visit to the sleepy coastal town of Antonio Bay and, under the cover of the fog, murder the townsfolk. It's good for a scary movie. There are a lot of creepy things hiding in the fog—it's always a good time to be careful.

Fog is an accurate description of how I feel I'm living my life right now. When people ask me how I'm doing, the most typical response I give is, "I feel like I'm living in a fog." What that means for me is this:

Things aren't clear,

The whole situation seems surreal,

I find that I'm not thinking as clearly as I normally would,

I don't have quite the energy that I've had in the past,

The future seems very ambiguous and dark.

I feel like I'm living in a fog.

Occasionally I'll have a little break in the fog and feel "normal." I realize that normal is a very relative term, but for me it means I feel more like my old self. We were eating at a familiar restaurant a while back and for the hour that we were there, I felt normal. The familiar can be very comforting sometimes. Another time we were doing some climbing in one of the preserve areas in Phoenix and for those couple of hours, out in nature, with the sun shining down on us while we were getting some good exercise, I felt normal. I even had almost an entire day not too long ago where, for the whole day, I felt normal. I haven't experienced that for a long time. But honestly, that's about it. For most of the time I'm in the fog.

A while back a friend asked me how I was doing and I gave him my fog line. A little while later in the conversation, he circled back around to that comment and said, "You know, I've been thinking about what you said that you feel like you're living in a fog. What do you do when you are in a real fog? You slow down, but you keep on going because you know that sooner or later you'll drive out of it."

For some reason that resonated with me. It dawned on me that this is not the time to get paralyzed and stop dead in my tracks while I wait for the light to shine on what the next step will be in my future. Rather, I need to keep moving—slowing down a lot, but moving nonetheless. It's been said that God can direct a moving ship a lot easier than one sitting dead in the water. I've got to be like a ship that keeps on moving.

Many things can cause us to move into a fog season of our lives. Any major crisis can be a set up for a fog season. It could be the death of a loved one, loss of a job, a health issue, a divorce. Interestingly enough, sometimes even *good* things can cause a fog. Things like having a baby, getting a promotion, moving to a new town, getting married. A fog is just a season of life where, for a while anyway, things don't feel quite normal and it takes time for us to adjust to what our new normal is going to look like.

But during those fog seasons there can be a lot of scary things that can start spooking us if we're not careful. Our mind and our imagination can take us to places we don't want to go and that can ultimately put us into the pits emotionally: "How will I ever go on without my husband?" "What will I do to keep a roof over the head of my family now that I've been laid off?" "How can we possibly afford all these medical bills that the insurance company isn't paying?" "Now that I'm divorced, how can I possibly work and be both a mother and father to these kids?" The list is endless, and I'm sure you can develop your own unique list based on the distinctive challenges of where you are in your journey.

In fact, you know what might be helpful? Make a list of the frightening things you're thinking about while you are in your own fog. I've left some space for you to write them down—and if that's not enough room for you— find some paper and keep on writing.

I'm in a fog right now and these are the scary things that spook me…

1. _____

2. _____

3. _____

4. _____

5. _____

You've been honest with yourself, so now let me be honest with you. My list of scary things that are spooking me right now are as follows:

1. How does a guy in his mid 50s find a new job? I don't even know where or how to begin.

2. How am I going to be able to pay the bills? We don't have a lot of debt, but even the thought of making our house payment is a little overwhelming right now.

3. How do I deal with some of the anger that I'm feeling towards myself and others? I don't want to get stuck in some unhealthy place where I develop bitterness in my life.

4. Now that I've lost my dignity and self-respect and I've been humiliated, what do I do to try and recapture a little bit of self-worth and personal value?

5. And if it's true (as people are saying, but I'm having trouble believing) that better days are ahead, how long will it be before I begin to emotionally embrace that and begin to believe it for myself? I don't like this foggy season and I would really prefer that it be over quickly.

It wouldn't be very helpful for you or me if we just stopped right here. One of the things I've already been sensing intuitively is that once I come out of this fog and life becomes a little more even-keeled, my *new* normal life is not going to be the same as my *old* normal life. That's just a fact I have to face. As much as we may long for those good old normal days, they are gone, not to be recaptured. In fact, they shouldn't be. We have to realize that just as there are seasons of the year, there are seasons of life, and when a new one comes, the previous one has to step aside. Our task is to figure out how to welcome this new season with all of its challenges and opportunities and say, "This now, is the new normal for me and I'm going to deal with the obstacles and fears that come with this time and I'm going to fully embrace the good things this season brings." Does that mean we don't mourn the things lost? No. Mourning is a consequence of the messiness of life. We deal with it. We go through it. Ideally, we come out stronger on the other side.

There is a Bible verse that comes in handy for me right now. For over thirty years, I have had a very favorite verse of Scripture. Some people call a thing like that a "life-verse." In other words, its meaning is so special and significant to you that it frames your entire life, not just a month or a year or a season. I mentioned my verse earlier—Jeremiah 29:11 says, "I know the plans I have for you, says the Lord. Plans for your welfare and not for calamity. Plans to give you a future and a hope." I love the way the Message version of the Bible paraphrases that verse: "I know what I'm doing. I have it all planned out—plans to take care of you, not abandon you, plans to give you the future you hope for."

God has a plan for me, and He has a plan for all of us. Sometimes circumstances can cause us to doubt that plan but that doesn't mean it's not real and ready to be revealed at the right time. And it's a *good* plan. It's a plan that affords us a *future* (even when we don't think we have one) and a *hope* (even when we are feeling hopeless). God *never* leaves us stuck in the fog. Eventually we will get out of it. We just need to keep moving, slowly for sure, but keep moving. Let's be careful not to allow ourselves to become paralyzed by those scary, spooky things that we think might be hiding in the fog.

God is so amazing. While writing this chapter I had to stop for a while and head out for an appointment. As I was driving, the mist was still around me, though not as thick. Then I looked up into the sky and noticed a faint blue patch beginning to appear. It was then that I realized something. The fog eventually does go away.

REFLECTION #6
SKIPPING STONES

"I am a firm believer that there is no place where God is not."

–Maya Angelou

"I will never leave you or forsake you. I am with you always."

–Jesus

According to the *Guinness Book of World Records*, the world stone skipping record is forty skips, established by Kurt Steiner from Pennsylvania, in 2003. Previously the world record is believed to have been held by J. Coleman-McGhee. He skipped a stone thirty-eight times on the Blanco River in Texas in 1992. I've tried skipping stones over the years, many times in fact. I think the best I've ever done was maybe six or seven times. Forty skips is a pretty amazing feat as far as I'm concerned.

Skipping a stone is an interesting exercise. From a distance, when you throw a stone across the top of a lake, all you see is the stone skim the surface, rise up into the air, travel a little ways, drop down, skim the surface again, and the process is repeated over and over. But what if we could slow down and magnify that whole process? What would we see? If we could film a skipping stone and then put it into slow motion and magnify its movement we would discover something fascinating.

First of all, as the stone lifts off the surface of the water you would be able to see microscopic droplets of water falling off the stone all the way until it hit the water again.

And second, the stone would always be wet. It would never have enough time to totally dry out before it hit the water again.

Hold that thought for a minute and let me share an idea with you.

Just because there is distance, that doesn't mean there isn't closeness.

Diane and my wife have been friends since fifth grade. That relationship spans over four decades. To this day Diane and Char talk weekly, and try and see each other annually. They live 1,000 miles away from each other but Char would tell you without hesitation that Diane is one of her dearest and best friends.

Just because there is distance, that doesn't mean there isn't closeness.

I think about this idea as well as skipping stones when I think about my relationship with God. I'm going to give you an analogy: if God is the water and I'm the rock, is there ever a time when I could honestly say that God is never with me, that He has abandoned me or forsaken me? Even if I'm away from Him (like a skipping stone sailing just above the water) He has still "attached" Himself to me and I'm still "wet."

Most of us seem to go through our lives focusing on what I would call the "big-ticket items" of life. Big-ticket items would be things like our relationships, careers, having children, buying cars or houses, seeing a bank account grow, and our health. What I've noticed over the years is that frequently when big-ticket items in life are touched in a negative way people can get angry with God.

When a relationship falls apart

When one of the kids gets into trouble because of drugs, sex, or alcohol

When we lose our job

When our health fails

When our bank account empties out

When they foreclose on the house

that's when people start going through a faith-crisis. They begin to question God and become upset with Him saying things like, "God where are you? Why are you allowing this to happen? I thought you loved me. How could you do this to me? Why are you hiding when I need you the most?" And all of a sudden, God can begin to *feel* very distant.

But is He?

Just because there is distance, that doesn't mean there isn't closeness.

This paradoxical idea becomes very important when we put our relationship with God under a searchlight. King David, whom God called a "man after my own heart"[53] experienced times when God seemed distant. "Lord, why are you standing aloof and far away? Why do you hide when I need you the most?"[54] "Why have you forsaken me? Why do you remain so distant? Why do you ignore my cries for help?"[55] "Why have you abandoned me?"[56]

That's distance.

Yet he also said "The LORD is close to the brokenhearted and saves those who are crushed in spirit."[57] And, "Where can I go from your Spirit? Where can I flee from your presence? If I go up to the heavens, you are there; if I make my bed in the depths, you are there."[58]

That's closeness.

An even greater irony is that often when we are *feeling* most distant from God (like a rock out of the water) that is when He is the closest to us (we're still always wet). Remember, He is *close* to the brokenhearted and crushed in spirit. We just need to become more *aware* of that fact—that He *is working* and *involved* in our lives during those times when He seems to be so silent and far off.

Right now, thousands of things are happening in our bodies of which we are totally unaware. Trillions of chemical reactions are taking place in every cell, every second. Electrical impulses are shooting across synapses. Hormones are surging through our bloodstream. Our bodies are breathing, thinking, metabolizing, calibrating, repairing, purifying, digesting, and circulating all the time. The amazing thing is—we don't give it a second thought. As important and as integral as all those processes are to our survival, most of us are totally unaware of what our bodies are doing most of the time.

Hold on to *that* thought as well for just a minute.

It's with appreciation that I give credit to Mark Batterson, pastor of the National Community Church in Washington, D.C. for some of the following ideas. In an online "Evotional" entitled *Finding God in Unexpected Places*, he shares some great insights.

One dimension of spiritual growth is a growing awareness of what the Spirit of God is doing in us and around us. Genesis 28 is a case in point. Jacob has a dream that becomes a defining moment in his life. It's a paradigm shift for Jacob. "When Jacob awoke from his sleep, he thought, 'Surely the Lord was in this place and I was not aware of it. How awesome is this place! This is none other than the house of God: this is the gate of heaven.'"[59]

That's a powerful statement: "Surely the Lord was in this place and I was not aware of it." Here's another way of saying that: "God was here and I didn't realize it." In that defining moment, Jacob saw God where he hadn't seen Him before. He was more in tune with God. His spiritual antenna went up a little higher. There were more blips on his spiritual radar screen.

Philip Yancey describes a growing awareness of God this way. "I envision the Spirit not so much touching our mundane lives with a supernatural wand as bringing the recognition of God's presence into places we may have overlooked. The Spirit may bring that jolt of recognition to the most ordinary things: a baby's grin, snow falling on a frozen lake, a field of lavender in morning dew, a worship ritual that unexpectedly becomes more than a ritual."[60]

Most of us are totally unaware of what our bodies are doing most of the time. In the same sense, as important and as integral as the Holy Spirit is to the work of God in our lives and on this earth, most of us are unaware of what the Spirit is doing most of the time. We're like Jacob before his encounter with God. God is all around us, He is continually working and yet so often we're unaware of it.

Have you ever seen an atom? I haven't either. They're tiny. But they are around us all the time. Atoms are everywhere even though they aren't visible or discernable. In the same sense, God is all around us all the time. We may not see Him, we may not *feel* Him, but He's there. If we could get our minds around that idea, I think it would help us a lot when we feel distant from Him. Because remember, just because there is distance, that doesn't mean there isn't closeness.

We're told in the book of Genesis that in the beginning the earth was formless and void. Where was God in this formless void of nothingness? God was doing His hovering maneuver. "The earth was formless and void. Darkness covered the surface of the deep and the Spirit of God was hovering."[61]

From that chaos, from that formless, empty, dark void, God brought order and a beauty that is beyond description. Well, guess what? Nothing has changed. God's Spirit is still hovering over chaos. He wants to bring order and turn the chaos of our lives into something beautiful. The whole of creation is a macro example of what God wants to do in our life. He hovers over the chaotic situations wanting to bring order and beauty to those formless and void places in our lives.

The word "hover" in the Old Testament is a fascinating word. In regard to *time* it refers to the split second before something happens and the split second after something happens. In regard to *space* it refers to the space right in front and right in back. I love the way Thomas Merton captures this concept. He says, "The Lord travels in all directions at once. The Lord arrives from all directions at once. Wherever we are, we find that He has just departed. Wherever we go, we find that He has just arrived before us."[62]

David describes it this way: "You hem me in behind and before."[63] I think that the word *hem* is probably one of the best word pictures of the immanence of God. Whenever I read that verse, I think about my parents tucking me into bed mummy style when I was a kid. They'd tuck one side of the blankets under my right side and then tuck me in on the other side—from the shoulders down to the feet. It generated such a feeling of security for me. I was hemmed in.

The *Message* translation of Psalm 139:5 says, "I look behind me and you're there, then up ahead and you're there too." In other words, the Spirit of God is where we have just been and where we are going. He hems us in on all sides.

One of the roles of a parent is to hover. If you have toddler, you know that is a dangerous age as they are learning to walk and stay stable on their feet. In a way, as parents, you do what the Spirit of God does for all of us— you hover around your kids to keep them from falling as they head towards a coffee table or the sidewalk.

The Holy Spirit hovers. He is right around you. He is right before and right after you. He is right in front and right in back of you. One of the names for the Holy Spirit in the New Testament is *Paraclete.* In a military context, that word refers to a battle formation where two Roman soldiers would stand back to back with their shields positioned in front of them. They literally "covered each other's back." They were protected on all sides. The Holy Spirit has your back covered.

A.W. Tozer said, "God is above, but He's not pushed up. He's beneath, but He's not pressed down. He's outside, but He's not excluded. He's inside, but He's not confined. God is above all things presiding, beneath all things sustaining, outside all things embracing and inside all things filling. That is the immanence of God."[64]

Immanence is a theological term which means: *"existing within or inherent in something."* God is inherent or exists within all of His creation through His Spirit. That doesn't mean that nature is God. It *does mean* that God through His Spirit is immanent within all of nature. Nature has the fingerprints of God's presence all over it. Creation is not God, but all of creation bears the stamp of God's presence. God is transcendent from His creation—He is separate from it, above it, the personal Creator of it all, but He exists within it all through His Spirit. There is no place that God is not, in all of His creation.

The idea of immanence is that the Holy Spirit is inherently here—He is everywhere, at all times, around us, hovering, constantly doing things on our behalf, of which we are often unaware. And there is no place that He is not. Again in Psalm 139:7, "Where can I go from your Spirit? Where can I flee from your presence? If I go up to the heavens, you are there; if I make my bed in the depths, you are there." Psalm 145:18 says it this way. "The Lord is near to all who call on him." The word "near" is used in the plural sense. It means:

God is near to us in every way imaginable to the greatest degree possible.

That's why even though we may *feel* very distant from God sometimes; the fact is He is near to us in every way imaginable and to the greatest degree possible. He is constantly working, doing things for us, on our behalf. We just need our spiritual radar tuned up a little bit to see it. Why? Because troubles and trials, heartaches and hurts can blind us to His working in our lives.

Let me get to my point.

I've felt very distant from God the past many months. Whenever I've sat down to read, I can't do it for very long. My mind wanders until I suddenly come back to reality with a jolt and realize I've been staring at the page for five minutes and can't even remember what I just read.

When I try to pray my prayers seem very hollow, empty, and void of life and power. I go to church but I don't feel engaged. Rather than feeling like a participant, I feel like an observer. I feel like I'm going through the motions of spirituality but not experiencing the vitality of it. Saint John of the Cross called times like these "the dark night of the soul."

There was a time in my past when this place I'm in right now would bother me immensely. I would feel guilty and think, I need to try harder, and I need to make myself read, pray, memorize Scripture (the aftershocks of that legalism thing, still reverberating forty years later). If only I force myself and keep disciplining myself, I'll get through this and pretty soon I'll *feel* close to God again.

Then one day I realized I don't always have to feel close to God, because even when I don't, *He is always close to me*. He is hovering around me, hemming me in, in front and behind, to the left and to the right, going before and following behind. He is as close to me as He could possibly be! I just need to start *looking*, being *aware* of His presence and working in my life and current situation, noticing His provision in little ways, His answers to small prayers. The irony is, as I have done that (seeking to become more aware of His presence) I've actually started *feeling* closer to Him. Not because I've moved towards Him but because He is always hovering around me. This is such a freeing thought.

One of the things we used to do with our kids when they were young was to encourage them to be on the lookout for what we called, "I spy God." These were times during their day when they would be aware that God did something for them, helped them, showed them something, worked in a situation. At night while we were having dinner we would share some of those "God sightings." It helped them become more conscious of the fact that God was always working on their behalf. Char and I have been keeping track of God-sightings in our life over the past months as we've gone through this very difficult time. It's been so encouraging because daily we have seen God working in our lives and situation.

Let me give you some examples.

There is a woman who has been providing us weekly with groceries and household items. She's been doing it for months. That's God working on our behalf.

I was providentially directed to something that helped cure a painful sciatica problem I'd been having for over a year. That's God showing me that He's still close to me.

There have been people we know who see us in restaurants and then quietly pay for our meal. That's God using someone to show us that He hasn't forgotten about us.

I sold a car (my fun, fast convertible) within 24 hours after posting it for sale. That's God saying, "See, I can do something for you very quickly when you need it done."

Char was provided a job that completely filled the wish list she had written down and prayed about. This was after she'd received a letter from the company telling her she wasn't qualified for the position! Again, the Lord was saying, "See, I can come through for you."

We received some money from a class action suit for inferior windows that had been installed in our home. That lawsuit had been going on for years and we had no idea when or if there would be any money coming from it, but it came now when we needed it. That's God saying, "I have ways of providing for you financially."

"Surely, (*absolutely, without a doubt, beyond question*) **the Lord is in this place** (*my life*)…" I just need to be more continually aware of it. What I find so exciting is that it's when the big-ticket items of life are shaken up and maybe taken away from us, that we can become more aware *of all the other things* God is doing in our lives, constantly working on our behalf. Yet most of us don't even see or are aware of all that He's doing because we're so focused on the big stuff.

"God's loyal love couldn't have run out, his merciful love couldn't have dried up. They're created new every morning. How great your faithfulness! I'm sticking with God (I say it over and over). He's all I've got left."[65]

And so while I go through this difficult time of transition I have found real strength in repeatedly telling myself:

Just because there is distance, that doesn't mean there isn't closeness.

Wherever I go He is already there.

I'm the rock and He's the water.

There's no place that God is not.

He will never leave me or forsake me.

And even though I may not *feel* close to God, He is sticking to me like white on rice.

That's pretty cool.

[53] Acts 13:22

[54] Psalm 10:1 *The Living Bible*

[55] Psalm 22:1, *The New Living Translation* (NLT)

[56] Psalm 43:2, *The English Standard Version* (ESV)

[57] Psalm 34:18

[58] Psalm 139:7

[59] Genesis 28:16

[60] *Reaching for the Invisible God*, Philip Yancey, Zondervan Publications, Copyright © 2001

[61] Genesis 1:2

[62] *Seeds*, Thomas Merton, Shambhala Publications, Copyright © 2002

[63] Psalm 139:5

[64] *The Attributes of God*, A.W. Tozer, Wingspread Publications, Copyright © 1997

[65] Lamentations 3:22-23, *The Message*

REFLECTION #7

THE SHELTER

I have a friend I've known for long, long time. For years he was a successful businessman. He and a partner owned a printing company. A number of years ago they sold the business and John went through a period of about six months where he realized that he had found way too much of his identity through his business. He was feeling lost, worthless, asking the question, "What in the world do I do now?" You know, over the years I've passed on to a lot of people that trite little saying that goes, "When God closes a door, He opens a window." But in fact—it really isn't trite—it's true. When doors close, windows do open. I'm not yet fully convinced of it for my own life right now, but I've seen it evidenced in *so many* people's lives over the years that I just *know* it's true. I'm just waiting for it to be true for me.

John found his open window. He started working in a downtown mission. A few years after he began working there the director of the mission committed suicide and John was made the new director. Today, he runs a shelter for the homeless in downtown Denver, and he loves what he is doing. John's house is in the suburbs but his heart is in the city. The mission has an old building they've been able to renovate and they are open seven days a week, 365 days a year. Their directive is to "Feed the hungry, clothe the naked, and preach the gospel." Simple, clear, direct. I like that.

They provide daily breakfast and lunch for the homeless. John estimates they serve about 40,000 meals a year. They have a day room at the center where folks can come in off the streets and get warm, sleep, or visit. They have five respite care rooms for homeless people who have been hospitalized but once released aren't yet physically able to get back out on the streets. They come to the shelter and stay until they are fully recovered. The center has showers and a washer and dryer where very soiled and dirty people and soiled and dirty clothes can be cleaned up. They provide clothes, coats, shoes, razors, shampoo, and a host of other items that help make the lives of the homeless more bearable. They conduct Bible studies and have a Sunday evening church service. About 85 percent of the shelter's support comes from individuals. They have half a dozen or so churches that support the work as well. Whenever I think about that statistic, I get sick to my stomach, not about all the individuals who are giving to the shelter, but about the fact that so few churches do.

I know church budgets are stretched thin. There is never a shortage of places where contributions can go and every church has its own special projects that it is committed to supporting. In most churches however, a very large portion of the annual budget goes to paying for and maintaining the church facility as well as personnel costs. Comparatively speaking, a small percentage of money goes to help with social needs and community endeavors. But caring for the lost and disenfranchised of society is a big part of what the church should be about. Jesus told us as much.

> "Then the King will say to those on his right, 'Come, you who are blessed by my Father; take your inheritance, the kingdom prepared for you since the creation of the world. For I was hungry and you gave me something to eat, I was thirsty and you gave me something to drink, I was a stranger and you invited me in, I needed clothes and you clothed me, I was sick and you looked after me, I was in prison and you came to visit me.' Then the righteous will answer him, 'Lord, when did we see you hungry and feed you, or thirsty and give you something to drink? When

did we see you a stranger and invite you in, or
needing clothes and clothe you? When did we
see you sick or in prison and go to visit you?'
The King will reply, 'I tell you the truth, whatever you did for one of the least of these brothers
of mine, you did for me.'"[66]

Caring for the "least of these" in society is to be a prime
emphasis of the church. Sometimes we seem to get our
priorities messed up.

I really like what happens at the shelter. For example,
there's a little old lady named "Miss Tina" who lives across
the alley from the shelter. She's eighty-four years old.
About six years ago she had to borrow some money. She
borrowed $600 from one of those short-term, payday loan
centers. For the last six years she has been paying $30 a
month on that loan and that is just the interest. She never
was able to pay down even a dime on her $600. In six
years she paid over $2,000 in interest on a $600 loan and
still owed $600. Can you believe it? I think there ought to
be a special place in hell for people who take advantage
of a little old lady like that. Well, the mission paid off the
$600 for Miss Tina and now she can have that $30 a month
to spend on something she really needs.

There's also a state representative whose office is right
across the alley from the shelter. Occasionally one of the
homeless men will defecate next to the wall of her office
and one of her staff members will call John and tell him
to come and clean it up. People don't seem to like it too
much when someone poops outside their office. John goes
and cleans it up. He simply says he's picking up shit for
Jesus, because Jesus has picked up a lot of his shit over
the years. That's why I love John. He's real and he's raw,
and he is reflecting the love of Jesus to some of God's creation.

I was down at the shelter serving lunch with John the
other day and was struck by the way he talks to the men
and women coming through the food line. First of all, he

knows many of their names. Some of them have pretty interesting names, such as "Boston," "Chicago," "Jersey Mike," "Kickback," and "Leprechaun." These names reflect where they're from or go along with their very colorful personalities (which come even more alive after they've hit the bottle a little too much). But with these men and women John says, "And how are you today, my friend?" My friend. He called these lost souls, *my friend*. I wish I had a recording of his voice that you could play right now, because these words on the page don't adequately convey the kindness, compassion, and connection of spirit that John has when he says it. The words, *my friend* are not just loving words, they are spoken lovingly.

In his book *He Still Moves Stones*, Max Lucado relates the story of a time when Leo Tolstoy passed a beggar. Tolstoy reached into his pocket to give the beggar some money but his pocket was empty. Tolstoy said, "I'm sorry my brother but I have nothing to give." The beggar stood tall and said, "You have given me more than I asked for because you have called me brother." Lucado then adds, "To the love starved, a word of affection can be a feast."[67]

When Jesus walked on this earth one of the things He was continually criticized for was His association with "sinners." In fact He was called "a friend of sinners" and believe me, the people who were calling Him that weren't saying it as a compliment. But at one point in His teaching He said something that should warm the heart of every lost and love-starved person that walks on this planet. He said, "I do not call you servants any longer….but I have called you my friends."[68] God calls us His friends.

If you've never been close to a homeless person I think there are some things you should know. They are very dirty. Their hands are filthy. They smell. Their hair is matted and greasy. They don't have many teeth in their mouth and most of the ones they do have are rotten. And as for one of the things on the inside that really matters—

their self-esteem or self-worth—they don't have much. The years of living on the streets, the mental illness they struggle with, the toll the alcohol or drug addiction has taken, the fact that they are shunned, ignored, avoided, and ridiculed, besides robbing them of their physical health, has also robbed them of their "inner" healthiness.

As I watched the interaction going on, I could tell that these men and women love John. They love him because they know he loves them and cares for them and calls them his friends. And he means it. Most of us will never have to endure the shame, humiliation, and hopelessness a homeless person lives with, but whether you realize it or not, in God's eyes, we are as lost, desperate, and hopeless as any homeless person living on the streets.

The truth is, every single one of us needs a friend. Someone that will come to us and say, "And how are you today *my friend*?" We all need someone who will accept us for who we are, where we are. Someone who won't judge us for the mistakes we've made in our lives. Someone who will put an arm around us and say, "It's going to be O.K. I'm never going to leave you and we'll walk through life together."

I love what Lee Strobel says in his book, *God's Outrageous Claims*. In the chapter "You Can Even Learn to Forgive Yourself," he writes: "I am engraved with the likeness of our Creator and therefore I ultimately belong to Him. I matter to God, because His very image is etched into my soul! This is the basis of my value. Though I am tarnished by sin, God nevertheless considered me worth loving. My mistakes don't destroy the image of God that was inscribed in me, so my errors can't eliminate the reason why I have value in His eyes. I know that Jesus is willing to pardon even my worst failures and because I know that He's forgiven me, I CAN forgive myself."[69]

There have been a lot of times over the past many months when I've felt like a homeless person on the inside. This whole experience has done such a horrible number on my self-worth—it's been so humiliating and isolating. My confidence has taken a strong hit. I see people from the church in restaurants, the gym, in stores and I cringe on the inside wondering what they're thinking and how they're going to respond to me.

Self-forgiveness has been an issue. Being able to accept the love and forgiveness of others has been an issue. Believing that God can forgive me has been an issue. It's affected my ability to believe that the future holds promise rather than continual despair. I've found myself frequently daydreaming about what life might be like a year or five years from now, and often when I do that the future seems dark and bleak and uncertain.

I frequently have to keep reminding myself of what Jesus told us to do—not worry about tomorrow but instead focus on today. I need to live for today. I need to see God's provision for me, today. Tomorrow has enough troubles of its own. I can think about those troubles tomorrow. While volunteering at the shelter that's one of the things I've realized about the homeless. They live just for today. They have to. They don't have a lot of promises about their tomorrows. In some ways I wonder if that isn't a mindset or a framework for living life that God wants all of us to have.

Jesus. He is the friend of sinners. He loves you. He loves me. The neat thing about it is—He means it—He really does. Right now, I'm so very glad that He is *my* friend and that, "my mistakes don't destroy the image of God that was inscribed in me, so my errors can't eliminate the reason why I have value in His eyes. I know that Jesus is willing to pardon even my worst failures…" It's like one individual said in an email to me shortly after my resignation: "I don't really know what to say to you other than you are still loved and respected by many. I know that God still loves you **and He likes you.**"

"Where does my help come from? My help comes from the Lord"[70]

[66]Matthew 25:34-40

[67] *He Still Moves Stones*, Max Lucado, Thomas Nelson Publishers, Copyright © 1993

[68] John 15:15 *The Amplified Bible*

[69] *God's Outrageous Claims*, Lee Strobel, Zondervan Publications, Copyright © 1998

[70] Psalm 121:1-2

REFLECTION #8

ONE-WAY TO HEAVEN, HALF-A-MILLION WAYS TO HELL

"The LORD is good to *all*; he has compassion on *all* he has made." [Italics mine][71]

There is a woman in Somalia
Scraping for pearls on the roadside
There's a force stronger than nature
Keeps her will alive
That's how she's dying
She's dying to survive

Don't know what she's made of
I would like to be that brave
She cries to the heaven above
There is a stone in my heart
She lives a life she didn't choose
And it hurts like brand new shoes

Hurts like brand-new shoes

There is a woman in Somalia
The sun gives her no mercy
The same sky we lay under
Burns her to the bone
Long as afternoon shadows
It's gonna take her to get home
Each grain carefully wrapped up
Pearls for her little girl

Hallelujah
Hallelujah

She cries to the heaven above
There is a stone in my heart
She lives in a world she didn't choose
And it hurts like brand new shoes

It hurts like brand new shoes.

–Sade[72]

This Reflection needs an explanation. It received mixed reviews from people as this book was coming together. Some thought it *essential* that I keep it in. Others felt it didn't need to be included. In fact, with one of our daughters, it even created a small faith crisis. *That's* why I decided to include it. As much as we don't like the feelings and unsettledness it produces, having an occasional faith crisis is not a bad thing. Having our faith shaken up to the point that we're forced to examine it more closely is a *good* thing.

This book is about an issue I have in my life that seems to clash head on with my faith and my belief in scripture. The reality is there are *many* issues pertaining to life and faith that are difficult to resolve. They don't have easy answers. But just because the answers aren't easy to find, doesn't mean we should ignore the questions. There is a Chinese Proverb which says, "He who asks is a fool for five minutes. But he who does not ask is a fool forever."

I have a lot of questions about my faith and God. The older I get, the more I realize life isn't as black and white as I once thought. Rather than life becoming clearer it actually is growing cloudier. Life seems to be playing itself out in multiple shades of grey. This Reflection focuses on one of the many questions I have.

Doubt

Uncertainty

Confusion

Fear

What do those words have in common? They are all emotions that in many Christian circles, people are being told they should not experience. This especially includes Christian leaders. Leaders are supposed to have their act together enough to have their questions resolved and doubts taken care of. So leaders *definitely* shouldn't be experiencing these emotions. And woe to those who do. It's important to toe the party line and not ever question. Or if you do, be sure you don't share your doubts and uncertainties with others, lest they betray you. I'm aware of a current situation where that happened to a vibrant, dynamic leader. He was struggling with some theological concepts and in sermons and articles he shared those struggles and questions. Had he kept his doubts to himself, he probably would be just fine today. As it was, he dared to be vulnerable, to open himself up to others. The end result was he was fired. Another victory for keeping the faith "pure."

If I sound a little cynical at this juncture, I am. Over the years it's been distressing to see how many Christians *accept* the faith but won't *examine* the faith. They *believe* but do so *blindly*. Many, if not most, evangelicals in America today have a faith that is simplistic, self-serving, and very naïve. But at least it's comfortable. And tragically, I think that's the kind of Christianity we are serving up and offering people today—a faith that makes us feel comfortable.

During my years as a pastor I enjoyed facilitating a discussion called, "Ask the Pastor." It usually was a forum held through our Women's Ministry program, but there were a few occasions when we had this type of dialogue during Sunday services. People submitted questions in advance or just spontaneously asked me about some spiritual or scriptural issue. When I met with the women, their questions often focused on work or family issues, husband and wife relationships, or parenting. But frequently the conversations would also turn to some heavy-duty theological topics. Those times were fun and challenging for me. I enjoyed having to think on my feet, and appreciated the opportunity to interact with people in a way that was outside the normal venue of preaching.

One of the things you discover after you've been in ministry long enough is that people's questions about the faith or issues concerning Christianity can generally be reduced to a handful of very predictable subjects. People seem to have a never ending fascination with questions like:

- Is Christ the only way to God?

- Why do the innocent suffer?

- How can miracles be possible?

- Isn't the Bible full of errors?

- Isn't the Christian experience only psychological?

- Won't a good moral life get me to heaven?

- Wasn't Jesus just a great moral teacher?

- Doesn't Christianity stifle personal freedom?

- Isn't Christianity just a crutch for the weak and helpless?

- Doesn't science conflict with the Christian faith?

- What about people who have never heard about Jesus?

- Why can't Christians agree among themselves?

- How could a loving God ever send people to hell?

I've offered my insights to these questions many times. Most often people have seemed relatively satisfied by my answers. These are challenging and valid questions and they deserve to be seriously addressed.

Over the years there has been one question that I've never had asked of me, at least not in this way, yet I think about it a great deal. It is somewhat correlated to the last question above: How could a loving God ever send people to hell? For me it is one of the greatest and most disturbing questions of my faith. I guess in one sense, it's a question wrapped in an observation, like an enigma wrapped in a mystery. However, I think it has profound ramifications.

Sometimes when I am working with clients in my life coaching practice, they get very bogged down in the details of a problem or situation. In doing so, the problem actually becomes bigger in their mind than it really is. So we stop and I tell them, "Let's take a step back from all these details and take the 30,000 foot view." In essence I'm trying to get them out of the forest so they can see the trees. When that happens they discover how to put their problem into a more sane and proper perspective. That's what I want us to do here—I want to take the 30,000 foot view of an issue. By doing so perhaps you'll understand why the idea of a loving God linked with the concept of hell, creates such tension within me.

My question centers on the character and nature of God. It is very obvious to even the most casual reader of the Bible that there seems to be a stark contrast between the God of the Old Testament and the revelation of that same God in the New Testament as revealed through Jesus Christ. It is commonly asserted that the God of the Old Testament is a God of anger, wrath, punishment, and justice, while the God of the New Testament as presented in the person of Jesus is one of compassion, mercy, forgiveness, and abounding love. The disparity between the two is so great that some have even gone so far as to suggest they are two different gods.

It would appear that this Being we call God is one of very intense, complex and, from a human perspective, seemingly very antithetical attributes. Personally, I accept the idea that God can be both a God of justice and a God of love, and that He can be both at the same time. As a parent I've been both a father of justice and love to my girls when they were young. Disobedience demanded punishment, yet it always came from a loving heart, deeply aware that there was nothing my girls could ever do that would make me stop loving them or not have them remain part of the family.

So I believe that it is within God's nature to be both just and loving. My issue comes with what that all means practically. Let me ask the question in a few different ways:

Is it possible that there is a characteristic or a part of the nature of God that casts a huge shadow over all of the other aspects of His character?

Or,

Is there an attribute within the nature of God that is larger, or more predominant than all the other attributes?

Or,

Are all of the attributes of God equal?

The way God is being presented today it would seem that most evangelicals (and many others for that matter) assert that fundamentally, first and foremost, God is a God of love. He loves you and me deeply, intensely, passionately, and desperately longs for us to be in a relationship with Him. By the way, I believe this strongly, and it was a key theme in my ministry and preaching for almost thirty years. It's a comforting thought isn't it? It's winsome, it's alluring, it's hopeful. But is it an accurate reflection of His character? Is love the predominant attribute of God that overshadows all of His other attributes?

One might be inclined to think so. Jesus said, "For God so loved the world that he gave his one and only son that whoever believes in him shall not perish but have eternal life. For God did not send his son into the world to condemn the world but to save the world through him."[73]

The book of I John simply says, "God is love."[74] Maybe love *is* the predominant attribute of God.

Then again, have you ever wondered how many people have lived on the earth since humankind began? I have. I don't know why that interests me so much, but it does. In doing some research you find it's actually hard to pin that figure down. Part of it depends on how old you think the earth is, how long you think people have been around, and if you are an evolutionist, how you define a human being (Homo Erectus, Neanderthal, Cro Magnon, Homo Sapiens, that kind of thing). But let's not get too hung up on that because the fact is the numbers back then would all be relatively small enough as to be insignificant.

Estimates of the number of human beings who have ever lived on earth constitute an extremely large range, with low estimates around 15 billion, and the highest estimates topping out around 125 billion. Many of the more robust estimates fall into the range of 90 to 110 billion humans. At the extreme opposite end, there are those who make the claim that more than half the humans ever born are alive today. That would mean that since the world's population today is around 7 billion, the entire human population to ever have lived on earth would be about 14 to 15 billion.

A gentleman by the name of Carl Haub has a fascinating article that is posted to the Population Reference Bureau website.[75] Mr. Haub calculates that, in fact, there have been around 106 billion births since humans first appeared, and therefore only around six percent of all humans who have ever lived are alive today. But you can see that there is a wide gap between the low and high estimates: 15 billion to 100 billion or so.

What does all this have to do with anything? It is estimated that about 2.1 billion of the approximately 7 billion people living on the planet today identify themselves as Christian, and that is a *huge* umbrella figure taking in all types of Christian denominations and beliefs. It is a number that includes Catholic and all Protestant denominations combined. But when we're all lumped together we do make up the largest religion in the world.

I also wonder how many people since Christianity began in the first century until now have been Christians. What number would you add to that 2.1 billion currently alive today? Five hundred thousand more? A million more? One billion more? Let's say we *double* the number and guess that since Christianity began there have been a total (dead and alive) of four to five billion people on the planet who believed in some way, shape or form in Jesus as the Son of God (which seems *very* unrealistic to me, but let's go with it for the sake of argument).

Then what about the very narrow evangelical view that only "born again" Christians will enter into heaven? Jesus did say "You must be born again."[76] And "I am the way, the truth and the life, no one comes to the Father but through me."[77] Of those four to five billion Christians, how many of them would be considered born again? Realistically, a very, very small percentage, but again for the sake of argument, let's say *all* of them are born again.

Just as an aside, since born again theology has only been around for about the last fifty years, I wonder about the millions of people who have claimed to be Christians down through the centuries who didn't have the benefit of our 20th century enlightened theology which spawned the born again movement. What's happened to all of them?

Here's my issue. Let's put some figures side by side:

Let's start by using Carl Haub's rather large number. Let's say around 100 billion people have lived on the earth. And just for the sake of argument, in case he really overestimated it, let's cut that number in half, to 50 billion.

The number of people to have lived on earth: 50 billion.

The number of Christians to have lived on earth: 5 billion. Remember, we're being really generous here and saying that *all* of those people have been/are born again Christians—the only kind that get to heaven, right?

Fifty billion and five billion. Ten percent of the world's population going to heaven and ninety percent of the world's population going to hell.

If you don't like the way that sounds, let's use the other very conservative number:

Number of people who have lived on the earth...15 billion.

Number of Christians to have lived on the earth...5 billion.

Fifteen billion and five billion. One-third of the world's population going to heaven, two-thirds of the world's population going to hell.

Either way you figure it, there are going to be *far more* people in hell than there are in heaven. I guess that supports what Jesus said [Italics mine]: "Enter through the narrow gate. For *wide* is the gate and *broad* is the road that leads to destruction, and *many enter through it.* But small is the gate and narrow is the road that leads to life and only a *few* find it."[78]

Either way you look at this issue, I think we have a conundrum. If we understand things correctly, hell is going to be far more populated than heaven.

Is it possible that the *justice* of God is the predominant part of His nature and the *love* of God is minuscule in comparison? The simple statistics would seem to bear out that conclusion.

So as I see it, evangelicals are left with a huge problem.

1. Maybe Scripture is not accurate in its presentation of the character and nature of God. Maybe God

really isn't a God of love. Maybe God isn't a God of justice. But that opens up a Pandora's Box for those who believe in the inspiration and inerrancy of the Bible.

2. Maybe there are other ways to heaven that we don't realize or understand, but that undermines the very teaching of Jesus Himself.

3. Maybe hell is something we don't fully understand and perhaps people aren't going to stay there forever. In other words, maybe it's not the eternal "time out" like we seem to think. Remember my comment about my own children? "Disobedience demanded punishment, yet it always came from a loving heart that was deeply aware that there was nothing my girls could ever do that would make me stop loving them or not have them remain part of the family."

4. Maybe as God's followers we are grossly misrepresenting and misunderstanding the nature of God and would do well to adjust our preaching and writing to more accurately reflect this God of justice rather than this feel-good God of love.

In thinking this through, I'm not sure if any of the above choices are attractive ones for the twenty-first century evangelical. I've tried to think of other alternatives but so far have drawn a blank. These aren't pleasant options to think about, and sadly what often happens when faced with challenging and difficult concerns is to fall back to a comfortable position, or the standard party line. We develop some semi-suitable answers, hoping that most people won't give an issue like this too much thought. Then we can move on to other, more important things. As an added bonus some may choose to brand those who raise an issue like this as heretics. A few centuries ago that would have resulted in being burned at the stake.

Along with my own personal struggle of trying to integrate my sexuality with my spirituality, this is just another issue among many that troubles me. It is a concern that has some incredibly profound implications were we willing to address it honestly and with integrity. So many issues and questions in life don't have easy answers. However, one thing I learned a long time ago is that when answers to questions are not forthcoming, they must be left in that foggy wasteland of the unknown. Perhaps this is one of those questions.

I think this is important to note: when faced with questions we cannot get our mind around, sometimes what we need to do is trust. I realize I don't understand everything and as the Bible says, "Now we see things imperfectly as in a cloudy mirror, but then we will see everything with perfect clarity. All that I know now is partial and incomplete, but then I will know everything completely…"[79] I don't understand it all, but then again, maybe I don't need to. I'm not God. I've got to be O.K. with that. Questions about faith should be addressed, not ignored. But in the end, God is calling me to trust Him as best I know how *in spite of* my questions and confusion.

As I wrote this chapter it dawned on me (somewhat late in the writing process, I might add) that there are three basic premises in this book:

The first is that simplistic answers to complex issues nullify the importance of critical thought. Simple answers may pacify some people but they do not help *thinking* people. I wonder if Christians have been guilty of simplifying life to the point that many in the world deem the faith to be irrelevant?

The second premise is that God is a whole lot bigger and more complex than we give Him credit for being. He is mysterious and His ways are often a mystery. We need to be willing to embrace this idea of mystery and live with the tension that mystery creates. It's been said that God made man in His image, and then man returned the favor. Often God is nothing more than a bigger version of ourselves.

The third premise is that since there are things we don't understand because of the complex messiness of life and the vastness of a mystifying God, we are called upon to trust and have faith.

When we look at conditions in the world and the history of the human race, there is little doubt that suffering and pain are an integral part of the human experience. Untold millions live in fear for their lives because of tyrannical and oppressive governments, watch their children starve or die from AIDS, are victims of natural disasters that destroy even the little they did have, suffer the daily pangs of hunger, and exist simply to try and live for another day. As Sade says in her song, people like this live in a world they didn't choose and there is a stone in *my* heart, and it hurts like brand new shoes. For them, is this life of suffering simply a prelude to an eternity of suffering? My mind and my heart cry, "No" but in the end I have to say, "I don't know."

Ultimately however, I choose faith in God. Everyone chooses to believe *something*. I choose to believe that God *is* love and that we are products of His love. I don't fully understand the messiness of this world. I don't have an answer to the question this chapter poses. I don't fully comprehend the complexity of my own life and sexuality. Yet I chose to believe, both in my life and in this world that God knows what He's doing. He knows what is going on. Nothing takes Him by surprise or catches Him off guard, and in the end He's going to make everything turn out the way it's supposed to. That belief gives me hope, even in the midst of the messiness.

I do have to tell you however, I'm very glad I'm not a pastor any more. Because in addition to sharing my personal struggle with you, I've also shared a big faith question with you, and I don't have to worry about being fired. Thank goodness I live in the twenty-first century. Being burned at the stake doesn't sound like much fun.

[71] Psalm 145:9

[72] "Pearls" by Sade from the album *The Best of Sade* originally released, 1994. Lyrics © Sony/ATV Music Publishing LLC

[73] John 3:16-17

[74] I John 4:8

[75] Population Reference Bureau website: www.prb.org

[76] John 3:3

[77] John 14:6

[78] Matthew 7:13-14

[79] I Corinthians 13:12 *The New Living Translation* (NLT)

FOURTEEN

ENGEDI

I'M WRITING THIS CHAPTER while spending some time down in Arizona. Through the kindness of some friends, we are staying at a guest house which is on their property. I wish I could show you a video of their place. It's unlike anything I've ever seen before in a private residence. The home sits on three acres, which are entirely walled in. From the street you can't even see the house or grounds, but once you pass through the front gate, you enter a totally different world. What makes this place unique is that it has its own well. They have their own never ending supply of water, which doesn't happen very often in the desert.

One of the things you notice when you go to Arizona is how homeowners choose to landscape their properties. Because of the intense heat and the fact that water is a very precious and expensive commodity, what you'll frequently find is a house that has no grass whatsoever. The entire yard is rock with cacti as the primary decorative plant. I can't say that it's very pretty—in fact I think it's downright ugly. It makes the landscape seem so barren and desolate. One of the things you realize when you're in a desert is you really need water to keep things alive.

It's funny how your mind will play irrational tricks on you once in a while. We almost moved to the Phoenix area about fifteen years ago. We made a couple of house hunting trips during July and August. This happened to be a year when they were having one of the hottest summers on record. The temperature hovered between 118 and 122 degrees day after day. Here we were looking at one house after another, getting in and out of a real estate agent's car that never cooled down, going into houses where an air conditioned 90 degrees felt like a relief. On one of our trips the agent's car battery died. We left one of the homes we were looking at, got in the car, she turned on the ignition and nothing happened.

This was before cell phones became such a necessity for our daily living (in other words, the agent didn't have one), so I got out of the car and began to push it down the road to a 7-Eleven a few blocks away where she could call a tow truck. I don't know why she didn't just go to one of the neighbor's house and ask to use the phone, but the agent, my wife, and a friend all stayed *in* the car while I pushed (you'd think at least two of them could have gotten out making things a little easier!) By the time we got to the station, I was completely, totally drenched in sweat. My shirt and pants were soaked and the whole time I was thinking "What in the world would possess a person to live here? The heat must have fried everyone's brains." But on one of those trips I found myself having the same thought over and over: "We're in the middle of a desert here…what if they run out of water…what will all these people do…how are they going to survive…they'll leave this place in droves and Phoenix will become a ghost town." We ended up not moving there.

Let me get back to our friend's place. When you drive through the gate you enter a little bit of paradise. The entire grounds are lushly landscaped. Green grass is everywhere. There are hundreds and hundreds of flowering bushes, trees, shrubs and plants of all kinds all over the property. They have a rose garden. There are waterfalls and fountains, walking paths, a putting green. It's like driving on to the grounds of a high end resort, but it's a private home. It's truly a little bit of heaven on earth.

As you pull up to the front of the house, one of the things you see is a sign leaning up against a tree. All it says is ENGEDI.

EN-GEDI.

Engedi is the name of an oasis which is located on the western side of the Dead Sea, close to Masada and the caves of Qumran in Israel. This is a part of Israel filled with incredible history and drama. The area surrounding the Dead Sea makes Arizona look like part of the Amazon. It is the most desolate place I've ever seen in my life. Nothing grows there. It's just rock. Miles and miles of barren rocky cliffs. It's a wasteland.

There is a monastery that is still in use today out in this desert. It's built into the side of a mountain and is very difficult to get to. It's for those people who really want to get away from it all.

Masada is the mountain where the Jewish people held off the Romans for three years as the Romans tried to subdue a Jewish rebellion. Finally after a three year siege, accompanied by the Roman army forcing Jewish slaves to build a huge stone ramp up the side of the mountain to reach the top, the Jews in the fortress of Masada committed suicide rather than be captured and killed by the Romans. They wanted to die free. It's a powerful story. In fact, to this day every new recruit into the Israeli army is taken to the top of Masada where they are administered the oath of allegiance and service to their country.

The Qumran caves are famous because that's where the Dead Sea Scrolls were found. These scrolls of some of the Old Testament books were among the most important archeological discoveries of the twentieth century. It's an area filled with historical significance.

But in the midst of all this barrenness, all this nothingness, there is Engedi, an oasis in the midst of the desert. It's known for its caves and springs of fresh water with a rich diversity of flora and fauna. Engedi is mentioned several times in biblical writings. For example, in the Song of Solomon it says "My beloved is unto me as a cluster of henna flowers in the vineyards of Ein Gedi."[80] According to Jewish tradition, David hid from King Saul in the caves at Engedi when Saul was pursuing David to kill him. "And David went up from there and dwelt in the strongholds of Ein Gedi."[81]

Our friends have an Engedi. Literally, it is like an oasis in the midst of the Arizona desert. However, it's more than that. With great grace and love and generosity, they have intentionally made an Engedi for people who are going through their own personal desert. For Char and me and many others this place has become one of refreshment, renewal, and restoration. It's a place of quiet peacefulness, of rich color and beauty, where a tired, beleaguered soul can come and find a shelter in the midst of a storm. In fact as I write this, my wife is out walking the grounds, reading her Bible.

Being here has made me realize something. Even in the midst of my desert experience, God has an Engedi. Let me personalize that for you: even in the midst of *your* desert, God has an Engedi for *you* as well.

An Engedi can take different forms:

• It might be a *person* who comes alongside and refreshes. One of the things you notice in the writings of the Apostle Paul is how many times he refers to the people in his life that refreshed him by their love and concern for him.[82]

There's one I'd like to share—it means a lot to me personally. "I'm sure you know by now that everyone in the province of Asia deserted me, even Phygelus and Hermogenes. But God bless Onesiphorus and his family! Many's the time I've been refreshed in that house. And he *wasn't embarrassed a bit* that I was in jail. The first thing he did when he got to Rome was look me up...." [Italics mine][83]

To have people in your life who are willing to stand beside you when many might be embarrassed to be seen with you is probably one of the most renewing and re-

freshing things a person can experience. At least it has
been for me. About a week after my resignation I received
an email from some very dear friends. I honestly wasn't
too sure how they were going to respond to the recent
revelation. Here's what it said:

> "Dear Paul,
>
> You are the same man today that you were a
> week ago who taught me truth from God's
> word; you are the same man I have respected
> for 13 years because of the man, husband and
> father you are; you are the same man that you
> were three weeks ago who came to our home as
> a friend and we laughed, cooked and shared
> stories together. Today you have one less secret/
> burden but you are still the same incredible man.
>
> We are all friends, heart friends, *no matter
> what*. (We) are here for you and Char and
> **always** will be.
>
> With love and respect,
>
> B"

To have men and women who have been willing to
stand beside me when many might be embarrassed to be
associated with me—people like that become visible mani-
festations of the grace of God. This has been especially
meaningful because in the months following my resignation, I was surprised by some of the folks I did *not* hear
from. Church leaders, staff members and individuals that
I considered to be good friends and thought we had a
significant relationship—I never heard a word from them.
That's hurtful, but their silence is revealing and makes
the support of others all the more valued.

Some people from Grace Chapel have been an oasis
of refreshment for Char and me. I alluded to this earlier,
but after my resignation we received hundreds of cards,
emails, and phone calls from people within our church.

Not a single one was negative or condemning. Rather the words they spoke and wrote were ones of love, mercy, compassion, encouragement, tenderness, hope, victory, grace, forgiveness, genuineness, concern, and kindness. If there are some from Grace who read this book, I want to say "Thank You." Their kind words have refreshed our souls during a very dry and difficult time. Even though I find myself somewhat disheartened at the state of the church right now, they have been shining examples of God's love. They truly have been people of *grace.* I am proud that they are living up to the name of the church I love.

- It might be a *place* that restores. In Psalm 23 David describes how God takes us to places that can be refreshing. "The Lord is my shepherd. I shall not be in want. He makes me lie down in green pastures. He leads me beside quiet waters. He restores my soul."[84]

"Being here makes our problems seem so far away doesn't it?" It was almost a rhetorical question Char had asked, as if she was musing to herself out loud. But it was true. Being away, enjoying the warm sun and peaceful surroundings really *did* make it seem like our problems were a distant memory. They weren't, of course. At some point in time you have to re-enter the real world, but the point is that *for a while* this place had become an Engedi, a place where our souls could be restored.

- It might be an *activity* that is renewing. Something that energizes us in the midst of our time of darkness and difficulty.

I happen to be a cycling instructor for a national fitness chain. "Spinning" as it is called, is a very intensive aerobic workout on stationary bicycles with a routine that is choreographed to music. If you haven't tried it, you really should sometime. It'll kick your butt until you get used to it. In fact, I *love* it when people walk out of my class and say, "Wow, you kicked my butt today." I get a big smile on the inside when I hear that. Over the months after my resignation one of the activities that I found to be very renewing was teaching my cycling classes. For that hour, three times a week I felt normal. It took my mind off my problems and I had 60 minutes of a renewing activity, both physically and mentally.

The important thing is this: When we are in a desert, let's look for an Engedi. Find that oasis that can refresh, renew, and restore. God hasn't left us in complete barrenness. Even in the midst of our deserts, He has an Engedi. And we need to go there and drink deeply of the refreshment that it provides. An Engedi is just another way God has of letting us know that He hasn't left us alone or forsaken us. They are tangible, visible, practical reminders that God is here, right now, with us, strengthening us, sustaining us—even through the driest and most difficult of times.

The following words encourage me, perhaps they will do the same for you:

"Don't be afraid, I've redeemed you.

I've called your name. You're mine.

When you're in over your head, I'll be there with you.

When you're in rough waters, you will not go down.

When you're between a rock and a hard place,

it won't be a dead end—

Because I am God, your personal God…

I paid a huge price for you:

all of Egypt, with rich Cush and Seba thrown in!

That's how much you mean to me!

That's how much I love you!

I'd sell off the whole world to get you back,

trade the creation just for you."[85]

In the midst of our deserts, He has an Engedi.

Thank you J & P. Thank you for being our Engedi. Your home and your hearts have refreshed us more than we have words to express. However, I do still wonder if someday Phoenix won't become a ghost town.

---

[80] Song of Solomon 1:14

[81] I Samuel 24:1

[82] Paul's references to people who refreshed him: Romans 15:30; I Corinthians 16:17; II Corinthians 7:6

[83] II Timothy 1:15 *The Message Version*

[84] Psalm 23:1-3

[85] Isaiah 43:1-4 *The Message Version*

 FIFTEEN

THE HARBOR

"If we don't change, we don't grow. If we don't grow, we aren't really living."

–Gail Sheehy

I LOVE CHINESE FOOD. It's my absolute favorite. In fact Asian food of all kinds is a real treat for me, whether Chinese, Thai, Asian fusion, or even Sushi (to a *limited* degree). It's all good. However, I don't put a lot of stock in fortune cookies. They're fun to read and whenever we're out eating Chinese food, our tradition is to all read our fortunes to everyone else at the table.

The day I sat down to write this chapter, my first thought, once I'd gotten settled and ready to write was, "I'm hungry." Sometimes it takes a while to get into the mood to write, and eating is always a great diversion, so I headed for the kitchen. Someone had brought over a meal for us and had included a handful of fortune cookies. That's where my taste buds went this particular morning.

I cracked open the first cookie and the fortune said: "You will continue to take chances and be glad." My thought was, how appropriate, because I'm just ready to write about that very subject. However, I was still hungry, so I ate a few more cookies. The second fortune said, "You will be rewarded for your patience and understanding." Not bad. The third read, "Good news will come to you from far away." O.K. now it was beginning to get a little too generic for me. The fourth one said, "You will be called to fill a position of high honor and responsibility." That's when I quit eating because I realized—no, that's where I just came from, not where my future is taking me.

I ate four cookies that morning but the first fortune was still the best: "You will continue to take chances and be glad." Taking risks is something most of us do at some point in our lives. We seem to be willing to take chances much more frequently when we're young and foolish. Sometimes, when watching TV, I'll tune in to a skateboard contest or one of those funniest home video shows. Some of the things I see on those programs literally make my stomach do flip flops. When I see a skateboarder jump and flip in mid air and then not land on his feet but instead splatter all over, that makes my stomach flip flop. When I see another one try to ride a rail and then slip off and fall right on the rail between his legs—oow—that makes my stomach do flip flops.

Crazy teenagers. You don't find a lot of forty year olds riding skateboards. There's a reason for that. For one thing we tend to become a little more concerned about protecting our manhood, if you know what I mean. But there's a bigger reason. Many years ago I realized that the older we get, the less willing we become to take chances. Instead, what we try to do is preserve our gains. We begin to live our lives and focus our attention on how to retain what we have accumulated, achieved, and accomplished over the years. We start playing it safe. Some people would call it living in a rut. In all honesty, ruts aren't that bad. They can be nice, safe, secure places to live.

But I once heard someone say,

"A ship in harbor is safe. But that's not what ships are built for."

To me, that statement is a much more profound way of saying, "You will continue to take chances and be glad." A ship in harbor *is* safe. But ships are made for the open sea. They are built to be out there—in the dark, forbidding, very deep and dangerous ocean. In fact, the only reason a ship goes into harbor is to drop off its cargo and then back out into the open water it goes.

I think about that as it relates to our lives. How many of us want to stay in the harbor and play it safe? And in taking that attitude, I wonder—are we missing out on a key ingredient in what it means to truly live?

I'd like to share a few stories from the Bible with you. They speak to this issue of staying in the harbor. Let's take Joseph as our first example.[86] Joseph was a very sharp young man. But as a teenager, he still had some growing up to do. There was the issue of how he handled some dreams he was having. He dreamed that one day his father would bow down to him and be in submission to him. He also dreamed that one day his many brothers would do the same thing. In youthful arrogance, he told his family members about these dreams. It didn't go over well and they didn't like him much because of that. But there was even a bigger problem. Joseph's dad played favorites. And Joseph was his very favorite, most loved child. He showered Joseph with attention and gifts that his other children didn't get. He coddled Joseph and spoiled him. Joseph didn't have to go work in the fields with his other siblings. He was allowed to stay in the house and take it easy. Can we say, "Recipe for disaster?"

Thus the stage was set for what turned out to be a very dramatic story. Joseph's brothers got so jealous and hateful that one day they ended up throwing him into a dry well. I'm not sure if they knew what they were going to do with him after that. But, when a caravan of merchants came traveling by, they sold him to those merchants and Joseph began a journey that would forever change his life. This caravan traveled to Egypt where they sold Joseph into slavery, to a man named Potiphar. Potiphar was a pretty decent fellow and soon Joseph's intelligence and integrity became apparent to Potiphar, who made Joseph the overseer of his entire household. However,

Joseph also had a big handicap. He was cursed with good looks. The Bible says he was "well built and handsome." That fact didn't go unnoticed by Potiphar's wife. He kept refusing her advances until finally one day as she tried to seduce him, he ran from the house, leaving her holding his robe. As a spurned lover, she got angry, cried "rape," and Joseph was thrown into prison. He remained in prison for fourteen years. Fourteen years in prison for a crime he didn't commit.

His dreams came in handy however, because it came to the attention of the Pharaoh that there was a man in prison who knew how to interpret dreams. Pharaoh was having his own set of weird nightmares which no one could figure out for him. So he called for Joseph, who explained the meaning of the dreams. Pharaoh was so impressed he made Joseph Prime Minister of Egypt. What a turnaround in fortune! He went from the prison to the palace in a very short period of time. It was from that position that Joseph was able to exert a tremendous amount of wise leadership, guiding an entire nation through a very difficult time.

I wonder how Joseph would have felt if one day while sitting in prison with his daily portion of gruel, he was given a fortune cookie that said, "You will be called to fill a position of high honor and responsibility." That would probably have given him a good laugh. My point with Joseph is this: it wasn't by his own choice, but Joseph was pushed out of his harbor of safety and security and thrown into the open sea. It was a sea filled with uncertainty, the unknown, danger, unfairness, and injustice. You name it. Joseph's ocean was turbulent. But God had to do that to Joseph in order to get him into the position He wanted him in, so that Joseph could be a benefit and blessing to millions of others. Life isn't always just about us.

Then there is Moses.[87] I love the movie, *The Ten Commandments*. I used to watch it as a kid. I had a video copy, then moved into the 21st century with a CD version, and I still enjoy watching it on television. And Charlton Heston was the best Moses I've ever seen.

Most people know the story of Moses. A little Jewish baby picked up out of the river by the daughter of the Pharaoh of Egypt. Raised in the palace, he was educated by the best teachers, and dressed in the finest of clothes. He truly was an Egyptian prince—a child of privilege. The problem was that even though he was a prince on the outside, he was still a Jew on the inside. And he couldn't stand it when he saw his people being enslaved by the Egyptians, beaten and downtrodden. In a moment of weakness and a fit of anger he killed an Egyptian who was beating a Jewish slave. That's when his troubles began.

He ran for his life out into the desert and that's where he stayed for forty years, tending the sheep of his father-in-law, since somewhere in that desert he met a shepherd's daughter and got married. Then the most amazing thing happened. One day, just a typical ordinary day, God met Moses, by way of the burning bush. God told Moses that he was to lead the people of Israel out of Egypt and into the Promised Land. He was going to be the great deliverer, and God would perform some of the most astounding miracles in order to make it all happen. After forty years of talking to sheep, Moses was a little out of practice being a leader. He was none too ready to take on this challenge, but when God calls you to do something, it's best if you go ahead and do it. Sure enough Moses led the people out of Egypt and around the desert for 40 more years before he died. Years ago I read, "Moses spent the first forty years of his life thinking he was a somebody. He spent the next forty years of his life thinking he was a nobody. And he spent the last forty years of his life learning what God can do with somebody who thinks he's a nobody."

My point about Moses is similar to that of Joseph. The great event of his life wasn't through his own choice; in fact his situation came about because of his own uncontrolled behavior, but the result was still the same: Moses was pushed out of his harbor (the wealth, prestige, luxury, and comfort of the palace) into a very dark and stormy ocean. He had a lot of time in that desert to think about what his life *used* to be like, and a lot of time to ponder the fact that for the rest of his life he was probably going to be nothing but a shepherd. But God was using that as a training time. It was a time to prepare Moses for the greatest challenge of his life, when God would take Moses out of obscurity and thrust him into the limelight, and he would be used to be a benefit and blessing for millions of people. Sometimes life isn't just about us.

Let me give you one more example. Daniel.[88] A seventeen year old young man who was taken captive by an invading army, carted off to a foreign country, and put among people who spoke a language he didn't understand. There in the great city of Babylon he was trained in all the customs and beliefs of the Babylonians. When I think about Daniel at seventeen, I can't help but think about myself at that age. I was in my first year of college, away from home, stuck in a little dorm room, and eating the most disgusting cafeteria food I'd ever tasted. And even though Indiana wasn't that far from Colorado, I felt as if I had been carted off to a foreign country. I was very homesick. I imagine Daniel was as well.

But he made the best of the situation and determined that in spite of the drastic change in his life circumstances he was going to stay faithful to his God. God honored him for that decision. In case you don't remember, Daniel was the young man who was thrown into the lion's den because he refused to bow down and worship a statue that the king had made. The lions didn't even touch him. God protected Daniel and *in his captivity* Daniel prospered. He went on to become a leader, a statesman, and an advisor to the king, and in that role he was used to be a blessing to countless others. I keep coming back to this idea that sometimes life isn't always about us.

My point is the same. Daniel had a change in his life that was forced on him. This wasn't his choice. He was wrenched out of his harbor and literally dragged out into an ocean filled with uncertainty and change with a future that looked very dark and bleak.

When I think about people like Joseph, Moses, Daniel, and many others I am reminded that because we all like to play it safe and stay in our harbors, sometimes God has to do some drastic things to get us out into the ocean. I don't think He likes it that much when we start playing it safe and we get too comfortable and secure. I know we don't like it that much when we are pushed out into the ocean. But as people, we are like ships and we aren't made to stay in the harbor. We are built to be out in the open water so that we can learn how to let God be the wind in our sails.

I was pushed out of my harbor. Painfully. Suddenly. Wrenchingly. It all happened so fast that I still shake my head in disbelief. Right now I'm out there, in the ocean, traveling to an unknown destination. But one of the things I believe with all my heart is that God is every bit as much *out there* in my future as He is *right here* in my present keeping me afloat *today*.

While writing this chapter I took a break and went out to lunch with a friend. We went to a Chinese restaurant. At the end of the meal I opened my fortune cookie and read, "You will soon receive help from an unexpected source." It was an amazing experience. Because right there in the restaurant, while my friend was still talking—I had an encounter with God. A glimmer of hope pushed its way into my heart. It wasn't very big and it didn't last very long, but I sensed it. In my spirit I felt it, and for a very brief moment I had the fleeting thought that everything was going to be O.K.

So right now, I'm keeping my eyes open for that unexpected Source

because my ship has left its harbor,
I'm out in the open ocean
and my journey continues.

---

[86] Joseph's story is told in Genesis 37-50
[87] The story of Moses is told in the book of Exodus
[88] Daniel's story is told in the book of Daniel

Final Thoughts

A DROP OF INK

I was driving down a street the other day and passed by a church. On the marquee outside was the following thought: "A drop of ink may make millions think." I'm not under the delusion that the drops of ink on these pages will be read by millions. It could be only a few hundred or a few thousand. Whether the reading audience is large or small, I do want you to know that what you have just read has been written with a lot of TLC: tears, laughter, and concern.

Because this has been *my* story it generated a lot of tears. As I wrote, there were many times when I had to stop, wipe the tears from my eyes, and regain my composure before I could continue on. Tears can often be very therapeutic. If for no other reason, writing this book has been good therapy for me. Even though there were days when I cried, it was necessary. Virginia Casey said, "Tears are like rain. They loosen up our soil so we can grow in different directions."

Growth is a fundamental part of our journey through life. Growth is healthy. Growth is necessary. Swamps are stagnant and besides that, they stink. Ultimately, it isn't what happens to us that matters, but it's what we do with what happens to us that really matters. I want to be the kind of individual who takes all the experiences of life—the good and the bad—and allows God to do something productive with them. I want to be better as I grow older, not bitter. Tears help that process. Maybe they've helped you as well.

Sometimes I wonder why I think about things the way I do. As I wrote some of these chapters, then read and reread them, I found myself laughing. I don't know what part of my brain has been cross-wired so that I think about things like Labradoodles or Skipping Stones, or the scary things that are hiding out there in The Fog. But just as with tears, laughter is an important part of healing the hurts of life. I love the comedy of Bob Newhart. His dry wit and somber faced "deer in the headlights" look that he always maintains while delivering his lines are classic. He once said, "Laughter gives us distance. It allows us to step back from an event, deal with it, and then move on."

I experienced a major, life altering, and traumatic event. It not only affected me but also my wife and children, my parents and friends, and thousands of people at Grace Chapel. At various points along the way, when overwhelmed with guilt and shame and pressed down with the realization of all the horrendous consequences that happened because of my personal struggle, laughter was good medicine for my soul. I hope you don't think that because I've laughed some along the way while writing this book that I'm superficial or simply shrugging off the severity of what happened. That's not the case at all. You haven't seen me during the long, dark nights when I've lain in bed agonizing over all that has transpired. But I think it was Jimmy Buffet who remarked, "If we couldn't laugh, we would all go insane."

Most of us need to laugh more than we do. Maybe you smiled as you read and that in some way we've connected. There is comfort and encouragement when we realize that we're not alone and that someone else has thoughts, experiences or questions similar to ours. We don't feel so isolated and it lightens our load. I would like your load to be lighter and your burden easier to bear.

Finally, this book has been written with a lot of concern. After being in ministry for thirty years I wonder what I have done to contribute to the anemic and often times irrelevant church that we see in America today. What guilt do I have as a leader in helping foster unhealthy attitudes and judgmental spirits in the Christians I had the responsibility to oversee? What blame is mine in leading a church that ultimately became a church I didn't feel comfortable in—because I realized I couldn't share my deepest secret with my congregation and believe that I would be loved and accepted?

It was about five years ago that I began to have serious reservations about how effective all my efforts really were. Yes, I was a good teacher. People responded well to my sermons. I was an adequate leader. But did I help people become the kind of men and women they *should* be? Men and women who were powerfully and strategically impacting their world for God; people who were experiencing a *life transforming and transparent* faith? How much did I help people develop a different paradigm on spirituality—a new view of what life in God is like? A view that expects and anticipates imperfections, one that applauds vulnerability, one that understands that godliness is something more than just the presence of good behavior and the absence of bad behavior? Was I really helping people learn to trust God to mature them from the inside out, by the power of His Spirit…in His timing and in His own way? Or were they coming to church (as I was) feeling the need to hide behind their smiles and spit-polished exteriors because it didn't feel safe to be real? Did I truly help?

I'm not sure I did. I tried to do my best with the information I had at my disposal at the time and the tools I had to work with. The church I developed was based on a pattern I had seen modeled for me. It was the way church was done. It was a church that was squarely in the center of mainstream evangelical Christianity. But something was missing. I began to realize that a key ingredient to a healthy spiritual life and the heartbeat of a vibrant, flourishing congregation is the need to feel free. To be able to experience the freedom to be who you are at any given point in your life, knowing that those around you would be willing to walk with you on your journey, expecting the best but understanding if the worst comes out.

A thriving church wouldn't be measured by the ABC's of current church growth theories (attendance, buildings, and contributions) rather it would be a community of people who recognize their own brokenness and together support one another in this most difficult journey of faith, without condemnation or judgment, believing that God, in His own time, would do what needs to be done to draw each one of us closer to Him. It would be a place permeated with the scent of grace as people experience the rawness and the realness of life together, applauding victories and acknowledging defeat, understanding that because life *is* messy and even with the best of intentions, everyone is going to occasionally slip and find themselves in a mud pit.

When everything is said and done, my biggest regret has been that I probably did more to comfort the afflicted rather than afflict the comfortable. Comforting those who are hurting is such an essential ministry and *so very* needed in this world of ours. However, there is a difference between those who need consolation because they are hurting and those who are simply comfortable. Too many Christians have a faith that fits like a well worn pair of favorite old shoes. It's not really providing much support, but at least it's comfortable. Many need a good kick in the pants to move them out of their complacency into action, service, constructive thought, and honest realism. But making that transition is going to hurt, like putting on a pair of brand new shoes, and I'm afraid many will choose to stay with the familiar. They will be content to want what they've always had, so they will continue to do what they've always done.

As a group, those of us who claim to follow the teachings of Jesus haven't done the best job of representing Him to the people around us. In part I think that is because we haven't allowed ourselves the luxury of thought. I alluded to this in, "One-Way to Heaven, Half-a-Million-Ways to Hell." We are too quick to accept simple answers to complex problems. Intuitively, people know that complex problems *don't have* simple answers. In fact some problems may not have any answers at all and we'll have to wait for the all-knowing God to reveal those answers. When we act like we have it all together, know all the answers and have no questions, people realize there is something bogus about that approach to life and therefore something disingenuous about us. That type of attitude comes across as smug, arrogant and simple-minded. Because life is messy, spirituality is going to be messy as well. Trying to pretend that it isn't, doesn't make it so.

Questions are good. Some questions may not have answers, but that shouldn't keep us from asking them. Just as with tears, we grow when we question. We move deeper into the experience of life and the challenges of living life when we are willing to move out of our comfortable, confining boxes and begin to get a little dirty as we wrestle with the difficult issues of life and faith. In reading this, I hope some questions have developed in your mind. A deeper hope is that you've been willing to wrestle with those questions. Even if you don't have answers, don't ignore the questions.

On the broader issue of the church and where it is at this juncture in history, I do have occasional, small glimmers of hope. More and more believers are growing disillusioned with the status quo of church life. The downside of this is that people are leaving the church because singing a few songs, listening to a sermon, and getting their weekly feel-good fix isn't addressing the deepest needs of their life. That's not good. The church must not be abandoned, but it does need some adjusting. I have hope as I talk with individuals and I hear them wrestling with this mysterious God and the deep matters of faith. I have hope when I see small handfuls of people meeting together exploring new options. I have hope when I see a few large churches that carry a lot of traditional baggage, attempt to deal with the difficult questions of life. They are trying to get their hands around *how* the church can help Christ-followers develop an authentic, healthy, and real spiritual vitality—in the midst of the messiness of life.

They are trying to do what the church in every generation needs to do: figure out how to bring the teachings of Jesus to bear on the challenging problems we face in our world—both personal and social, and at the same time point people's attention to the promise of a reality beyond the one we now experience. The hope I have is found in a new generation of young Christian leaders who are moving towards embracing and grappling with these issues rather than continuing to seek the comfortable shelter of traditional boxes which make us feel safe and secure.

I don't know if there will be an opportunity for me to be a part of that dialogue in the future or not. At this point and for this season of my life, I focus on living a day at a time. I focus on the love of my wife who has stayed by my side and been a continual source of hope and encouragement. I focus on the love and acceptance of my children and my parents and the handful of faithful friends who have walked with me through this dark valley. And I focus on God. I love Him. I don't understand Him, yet I know He is the Source of life. Truly,

> "He alone is my rock and my salvation;
>   he is my fortress, I will never be shaken."[89]

I also want you to have hope. I know many of you wrestle with issues you feel unable to share with others or are afraid to have exposed. I've taken a step and put myself out there for the world to see. Perhaps it will give you the courage to do so as well. If nothing else, I want you to know I'm here for you. Rejection is not in my vocabulary. If I can listen, pray, share life over a cup of coffee, have an e-mail conversation, or somehow encourage you to keep on keeping on and not give in to despair—it would be an honor for me to be your friend.

I leave you with the following words: "Recipe for greatness: To bear up under loss, to fight the bitterness of defeat and the weakness of grief, to be victor over anger, to smile when tears are close, to resist evil men and base instincts, to hate hate and to love love, to go on when it would seem good to die, to seek ever after the glory and the dream, to look up with unquenchable faith in something evermore about to be, that is what any man can do, and so be great."[90] Dare to be great. Dare to believe and have hope. And on your journey through life, go with God, my friend.

> "Be strong and courageous. Do not be discouraged, for the LORD your God will be with you wherever you go."[91]

---

[89]Psalm 62:2
[90]Zane Grey (1875-1939)
[91]Joshua 1:9

A personal note. . .

It would be an honor to hear from you and I would enjoy receiving your thoughts on *Skipping Stones*. If you have found insights in the book—challenging, thought-provoking, hopeful—please let others know.

Thank you.

Paul

To book Paul for a speaking engagement, contact him at:

Paul@SkippingStonesBook.com

If you would like to interact with Paul and others regarding *Skipping Stones* or share your comments about the book, log on and blog at:

www.SkippingStonesBook.com